THE ALGORITHMS OF LIFE

How Nature's Oldest Code Is Shaping the Future of AI

A Nine-Chapter Exploration of the Parallels
Between Nature, Mind, and Machine Intelligence
with reflections on ancient wisdom, mandalas & sūtras

A NINE-CHAPTER JOURNEY BY

ABHIK BISWAS

notionpress.com

INDIA • SINGAPORE • MALAYSIA

ISBN

Paperback 979-8-90479-892-5

Hardcase 979-8-90560-817-9

Contents

Preface

Nature is the original engineer, the most patient scientist, and the most relentless innovator the world has ever known. For nearly four billion years, it has been running a continuous, planet-scale experiment in survival, adaptation, intelligence, and resilience. Every living thing you have ever seen is the result of countless iterations, failed prototypes, successful heuristics, and elegant solutions that no human research lab could ever match in speed, scale, or sophistication.

Artificial Intelligence, by comparison, is in its infancy. Though the pace of progress over the past decade has been breathtaking, AI is only just beginning to uncover the fundamental principles that nature figured out long ago. Many of our most exciting breakthroughs — deep learning, reinforcement learning, evolutionary algorithms, swarm systems, multi-agent architectures — are not really new discoveries. They are rediscoveries. They are the technological echoes of patterns that living systems have been running for eons.

This book is an invitation to look at those patterns. Across nine chapters, we will travel through evolution, cellular communication, swarm behaviour, neural plasticity, the immune system, ecosystems, philosophy, synthesis, and the wider family of Eastern wisdom traditions — Indian, Chinese, Japanese, and Buddhist lineages that quietly anticipated many of the structural moves that modern AI is now rediscovering. Along the way, we will examine how each of these systems maps onto a specific thread of AI — and what each still has to teach us.

The book is written for two audiences at once. The first is the technology expert — the engineer, researcher, architect, or founder who wants a concise but rigorous framing of the nature-AI parallels without the usual mathematical overhead. The second is the curious reader from any background who senses that something profound is happening at the intersection of life and machines, and wants a clear map of the territory.

You will not need a biology degree or a machine-learning PhD to follow along. You will, however, need a willingness to hold two perspectives at once: the wet, warm, wonderfully messy logic of living systems, and the dry, formal, deeply elegant logic of computation. The thesis of this book is simple: they are the same logic, wearing different uniforms.

How to Use This Book

Each chapter is self-contained and follows the same shape. You will find a short opening image, a main argument presented in plain language, a "Key Insight" box you can carry away, and then two companion pages: a NOTES page with ruled lines for your own marginalia, and a MANDALA page — a Buddhist design to color, with a short, gentle note on where it comes from and what it means. No background in any Eastern philosophy is assumed anywhere in this book. Anything that might be unfamiliar is explained the first time it appears.

The ninth chapter is a new kind of detour. Having spent eight chapters reading nature as code, we turn to a wider family of traditions — classical Indian, Chinese, Japanese, and Buddhist thought — that has been describing the structure of language, inference, attention, and action for more than two thousand years. The chapter is written to be approachable for a reader with no prior exposure to Sanskrit, Chinese, or any Eastern philosophy. A short spiritual reflection follows it, as a quieter companion to the more technical material.

By the final page, my hope is that you will see intelligence not as something humans invented, but as something nature has been practising for a very long time — and that you, as a builder, thinker, or leader, will come away with a sharper intuition for where machine intelligence is heading.

A Personal Note

I wrote this book in the margins of working days spent building real AI systems. The arguments here are not abstractions drawn from a conference circuit; they are the product of staring at evolving models in production and wondering what the older designers of intelligence — the forests, the cells, the nervous systems, and the ancient commentaries on mind from South, East, and Southeast Asia — would have done differently. The chapters are short by design. This book is meant as a map, not a library; the further-reading list at the back points to the deeper volumes.

Let us begin.

–Abhik Biswas

About the Author

Abhik Biswas is a technologist and systems thinker working at the intersection of nature, logic, cognition, and artificial intelligence. His professional practice spans mainframes, cloud native platforms, agentic AI systems, enterprise-grade quality-engineering architectures, and the design of intelligent software that behaves more like an adaptive organism than a rigid machine.

Over more than two decades of engineering leadership, he has observed a consistent pattern: the software systems that endure, scale, and self-correct are the ones that borrow, knowingly or not, from the logic of living systems. That observation has slowly matured into the thesis of this book.

He writes to bridge scientific insight with practical engineering — translating ideas from evolutionary biology, neuroscience, complex science, and the classical Asian traditions into vocabulary that engineers, product leaders, and executives can use in real decisions. His work is guided by a single belief: that the next generation of intelligent systems will not be built by copying nature's surface features, but by internalising its deeper patterns of adaptation, cooperation, and emergence — and that the oldest human traditions of inquiry, from the Indian sub-continent to China and Japan, still have something fresh to say about how to do that well.

The book you are holding follows that belief into nine chapters on nature and AI, a new ninth chapter on Eastern wisdom traditions, a short spiritual reflection, nine Buddhist mandalas to color in, and a ruled notes page after every chapter for your own working.

Introduction

Why Nature Is the Blueprint for AI

If you were asked to design a system that could sense its environment, learn from experience, coordinate with millions of peers, defend itself against unknown threats, repair its own damage, and continue operating for billions of iterations without a central controller, you would probably describe it as science fiction. And yet, a simple colony of ants — or a single human immune system — does exactly that, every day, without fanfare.

This is the puzzle at the heart of this book. The things we are just beginning to build in silicon have been running, at scale and at speed, in nature for a very long time. When a modern machine-learning system learns to play a game through self-play, it is repeating, in faster time, what evolution has done for millennia. When a distributed micro-services architecture routes around a failed node, it is re-enacting the improvisational brilliance of an ant trail repairing itself after a rainstorm. When a large language model forms a long-term memory, it is reaching toward a capability that neurons invented long before computers existed.

Once you begin to notice these parallels, you cannot un-notice them. The history of AI is, in large part, a history of engineers and scientists looking at the living world, extracting a principle, and encoding it into software. The term "neural network" is not metaphor; it is lineage. The phrase "genetic algorithm" is not a flourish; it is a direct lift. "Swarm optimization" is literally named for the insects that inspired it.

What This Book Will Do

Each chapter takes one pattern from nature and one strand of AI, places them side by side, and asks three questions:

- What is the underlying algorithm — the principle, the pattern, the repeatable logic?
- Where do we see it already inside modern AI, often without naming it as such?
- Where has nature gone that AI has not yet followed — and where might the next breakthrough come from?

The goal is not to flatten nature into a set of engineering tips. Living systems are infinitely richer than any algorithm we extract from them. The goal is the opposite: to use nature as a mirror, so that when we look at our own technology, we see it more clearly.

The Shape of Each Chapter

Every chapter opens with a short image, makes its argument in plain language, and ends with a Key Insight — a single compressed line you can take with you into your next design review, research paper, or strategy document. Then every chapter has two companion pages. The first is a NOTES page with ruled lines; if you are reading to put the ideas to work, that is where your marginalia belong. The second is a MANDALA page — a Buddhist design to color — paired with a short, plain-language note on where it comes from and what it means. You will not need any background in Eastern philosophy to enjoy the mandalas. Everything that might be unfamiliar is explained the first time it appears.

The New Ninth Chapter and a Spiritual Pause

This edition adds a ninth chapter on the wider family of Eastern traditions — Sanskrit grammar and the theory of attention in yoga, the Bhagavad Gita on the ethics of action, classical Indian logic, Confucius on the rectification of names, the Dao De Jing on non-forcing, the binary patterns of the I Ching, and the Chan/Zen disciplines of beginner's mind and koan practice. It is placed there not to bolt mysticism onto engineering, but because these traditions turn out to have anticipated, with startling precision, several patterns we are now rediscovering inside modern AI. A short reflection — "A Spiritual Dimension" — follows the ninth chapter, as a quieter counterpoint to the rest of the book.

How to Read This Book

The chapters are self-contained. You can read them in order for a cumulative argument, or dip into whichever one speaks to your current project. Use the notes pages as you go, and use the mandalas to slow the reading down when it starts to feel rushed.

A Word on Language

You will meet a handful of Sanskrit, Chinese, and Japanese words in this book, mostly in the ninth chapter. Every single one is introduced in plain English first. There is no glossary test at the end. If a term feels dense, you can read past it — the surrounding sentence will carry the meaning. The point is never to showcase the vocabulary. The point is to show that, for a long time, careful people in different parts of the world have been sketching the same diagrams for how minds work, and that some of those diagrams are uncannily close to the ones we now draw on whiteboards in AI research meetings.

What This Book Is Not

This book is not a textbook. It will not give you the mathematics behind gradient descent, the full architecture of a transformer, or the derivation of a population-genetics model. Those books already exist, and they are good. This book is also not a manifesto.

It does not claim that nature is always right, that ancient wisdom is always better, or that modern technology is always missing the point. The natural world sometimes does things inefficiently. Ancient texts sometimes say things that have not held up. Modern AI sometimes arrives at answers that nature never bothered with. What this book is interested in is the places where the three ways of thinking rhyme — and what those rhymes reveal about where we are going.

Three Habits I Will Ask You to Bring

First, curiosity across disciplines. Most of the interesting questions at the nature-AI boundary sit in the gaps between departments. Second, a willingness to hold two seemingly opposed ideas without forcing an early synthesis — a cell is both chemistry and computation; attention is both a mathematical operation and an inner discipline. Third, patience with slowness. The spiritual and reflective parts of this book are deliberately quieter than the technical parts. They are not filler. They are where some of the most useful thinking tends to happen, if we let it.

> **A FAIR OBJECTION, ANSWERED EARLY**
>
> "Isn't comparing AI to nature just a metaphor?" It can be, when used loosely. In this book, every comparison is tied back to a concrete algorithmic pattern — an optimisation loop, a message-passing structure, a feedback control law. If a comparison cannot survive that reduction, it does not belong in the argument. That is the only guardrail I hold myself to. Everything else is an invitation to wonder.

A Short Timeline of Ideas

It can help to keep a rough timeline in view as you read. The dates below are approximate; the point is the shape, not the precision.

- Around 3.8 billion years ago — the first self-copying molecules on Earth. The evolutionary loop begins.

- Around 600 million years ago — the first nervous systems. Signal, response, memory begin to form in tissue.
- Around 1000 BCE to 200 CE — across Asia, careful descriptions of language, reasoning, attention, and action appear almost simultaneously: the I Ching's binary hexagrams in China; Confucius on the rectification of names; Laozi's Dao De Jing on non-forcing action; Panini's Sanskrit grammar, the Nyaya school of logic, Pingala's binary prosody, the Bhagavad Gita, and the Yoga Sutras of Patanjali in India — all describing structures modern AI would recognise.
- 1850s — Darwin and Wallace articulate natural selection. For the first time, evolution is stated as an algorithm rather than a mystery.
- 1940s — McCulloch and Pitts publish the first mathematical model of a neuron. The term "neural network" is born.
- 1950s to 1970s — the first genetic algorithms, the first cellular automata, the first serious immunological theory. Nature's logic begins to be programmed.
- 1990s to 2010s — ant-colony optimisation, particle swarms, and neuromorphic hardware make the nature-to-AI translation industrial.
- 2010s to today — deep learning, transformers, reinforcement-learned agents, and swarms of language models put the whole story back into the spotlight — and back into a debate about what, if anything, we are still missing.

You can hold this loose chronology in one hand and the contemplative traditions in the other. Neither one is a prerequisite for the other. Both of them, together, give a fuller picture than either one alone.

KEY INSIGHT

Nature is the world's oldest R&D lab. AI is finally learning to read its documentation.

CHAPTER 1

The Hidden Algorithms of the Natural World

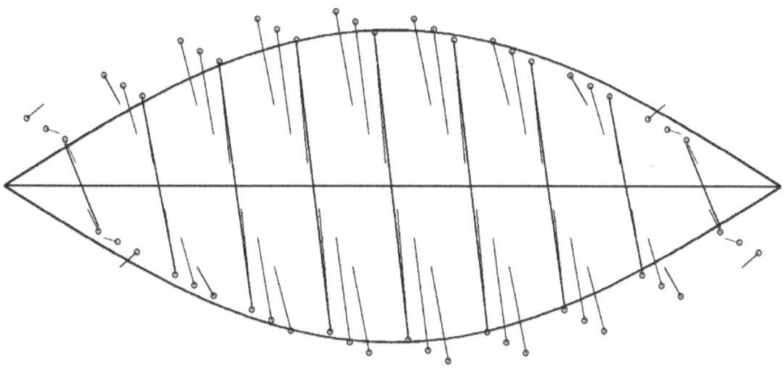

The leaf as circuit: nature's original board layout.

Step outside on a quiet morning. A bee is working a flower. A leaf is bending toward the light. Somewhere, a swallow is correcting its course mid-flight without thinking about it. Now ask yourself a slightly strange question: what, exactly, is doing the computing here?

This is the question we will keep coming back to. Nature is not just an inspiration for engineers. It is itself a computational system — the oldest one we know about, by a very wide margin. Every organism you have ever seen, every ecosystem you have ever walked through, is the live output of an algorithm that has been running without interruption since life began. The inputs are energy and information. The outputs are form, behavior, and survival.

If that sounds like a poetic flourish, it is not meant to be. It is increasingly how biologists, physicists, and computer scientists describe what they are actually studying. A cell, on a careful look, is an information-processing unit. A genome is a program. An ecosystem is a distributed system with no single owner. And as we will see in chapter 2, even evolution itself — the thing that produced the cell and the genome and the ecosystem — turns out to be a recognisable algorithm.

Biomimicry: Reading Nature's Blueprints

Start with a story you may have heard but is worth telling again. The Shinkansen bullet train in Japan was, for a while, a mild engineering disaster. When it shot out of a tunnel at full speed, the air it had been pushing in front of it would burst out the other side with a noise like a small explosion. Neighbours complained. The engineers tried the obvious things — more aerodynamic theory, fancier nose shapes — and got nowhere. Then one of them, a birder, suggested they look at a kingfisher.

A kingfisher dives head-first from air into water without a splash. Its beak is shaped to slice from one fluid into another while disturbing as little as possible. The Shinkansen engineers reshaped the train's nose to look like that beak. The sonic boom went away. As a bonus, the train ran faster on less power.

Owl feathers, equally, inspired the design of the train's pantograph to quiet the noise at the wire interface. The lotus leaf has inspired self-cleaning surfaces. Gecko feet have inspired dry adhesives. Termite mounds have inspired passive cooling. The pattern keeps repeating: a problem that human engineers are sweating over has already been solved — quietly, and for free — by a living system that has no idea it is doing engineering.

From Biomimicry to Bio-Computation

Biomimicry copies nature's shapes and surfaces. Bio-computation goes a layer deeper. It asks a different question: what is the underlying algorithm that nature is running? Once you can write that algorithm down in general terms, you can run it on any substrate — including silicon.

That is the path many foundational ideas in AI have actually taken. Nearly every one of these is something we will explore later in the book:

- Genetic algorithms encode the logic of natural selection (chapter 2).
- Neural networks encode a simplified version of synaptic communication (chapter 4).
- Ant colony optimisation encodes the pheromone-based routing logic of real ants (chapter 3).
- Reinforcement learning encodes the dopamine-style feedback loops found in animal learning.
- Immune-system-inspired anomaly detection encodes the self/non-self discrimination of T-cells (chapter 5).

In each case, the human insight was not to copy the animal. It was to read the algorithm underneath the animal — and then write that algorithm in a form a machine can run.

Three Recurring Patterns

Before we dive in, three patterns are worth naming up front. They will keep showing up — in the swarm chapter, in the brain chapter, in the immune chapter, in the ecosystem chapter — so it is helpful to have a name for them now. Think of them as load-bearing ideas you can hang the rest of the book on.

1. **Local Rules, Global Behavior**

   There is rarely a central conductor in nature. A forest has no CEO. A bee colony has a queen, but she does not decide which flowers anyone visits. Complexity arises because many small agents follow simple local rules, and their interactions produce a large-scale behaviour no single agent understands. We will see this idea up close in chapter 3, when we look at swarms — and again in chapter 6, when we look at ecosystems.

2. **Redundancy and Graceful Degradation**

   Nature almost never builds a single point of failure. Most biological systems have deep redundancy, overlapping pathways, and the ability to degrade gracefully under stress. A human brain can lose entire regions and still function. A forest can lose many species and still be a forest. Most software systems are the opposite — they fall over the moment a critical component goes down. The immune system in chapter 5 is a beautifully redundant defence; we will steal a few of its tricks for cybersecurity.

3. **Feedback Loops Everywhere**

   Every stable biological system is held together by feedback. Hormonal loops regulate metabolism. Predator-prey dynamics regulate population. Synaptic strength adjusts in response to activity. Remove the feedback, and the system breaks. Modern AI is slowly learning this: the systems that keep learning and keep correcting themselves are qualitatively different from those trained once and deployed. We will return to this idea repeatedly — most directly in chapter 4 (the brain), chapter 6 (ecosystems), and chapter 8, where it becomes the unifying loop of the whole book.

DID YOU KNOW

The concept of "algorithm" predates computers by more than a thousand years. The word itself derives from the 9th-century Persian mathematician al-Khwarizmi. Nature, however, has been running algorithms for roughly four billion years — so every engineer working with AI today is, in a sense, late to the party.

Why This Matters for Engineers and Leaders

If you are building technology in 2026 and beyond, here is the practical takeaway. The designs that will scale, adapt, and survive are the ones that treat nature's principles as a first-class reference architecture, not a cute metaphor. Distributed systems that can self-heal, AI agents that can cooperate, models that can keep learning after deployment — these are not speculative ideas. They are patterns biology already demonstrates at scale, and our industry is steadily learning how to implement.

The rest of this book is a guided tour through those patterns. By the time you reach chapter 8, the goal is for the underlying loop to have become almost obvious. You will see it everywhere.

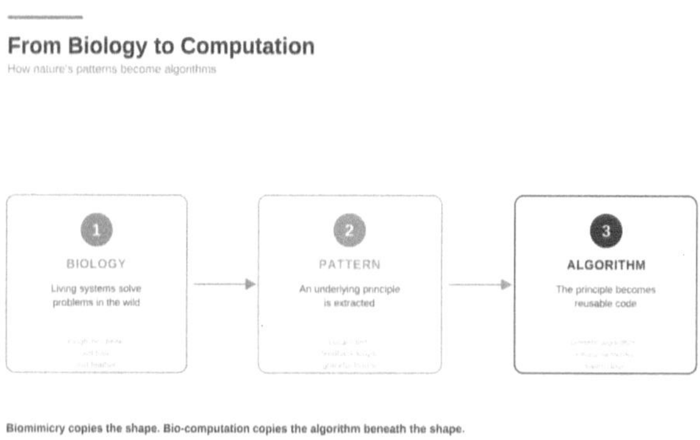

From nature to computation: every living pattern has a software counterpart.

> **KEY INSIGHT**
>
> ***Nature is not metaphor for AI. It is blueprint.***

Questions to Carry Forward

A short set of prompts to sit with before you turn the page. They are meant for your own use — in conversation with a colleague, in a margin, or on the notes page that follows.

- Where in your own work do you already see local rules producing global behavior?
- Is your current system redundant, or is there a single point of failure you have been tolerating?
- Name one feedback loop in your organisation that is silently shaping behavior.
- If you treated nature as a first-class reference architecture, which design would you change this quarter?
- What is one pattern in the natural world that you admire but have not yet tried to formalise?

CHAPTER 1 · NOTES

The Hidden Algorithms of the Natural World

What stood out? What do you want to come back to? Where does this show up in your own work?

CHAPTER 1 · MANDALA FOR COLORING

A pause to play: bring these ideas to life with your own colors.

Biomimicry: observing nature, then building with what it teaches.

Origin & Meaning

The Wheel of Dharma (Dharmachakra)

This eight-spoked wheel is one of the oldest symbols of Buddhism. It appears carved onto stone pillars across India from around 250 BCE. The eight spokes stand for eight practices the Buddha is said to have taught as a way to live well: right view, intention, speech, action, livelihood, effort, mindfulness, and concentration. The wheel itself represents setting a journey in motion — a fitting image for a book that invites us to see the hidden patterns inside the living world.

CHAPTER 2

Evolution as Computation: DNA, Mutation and Digital Intelligence

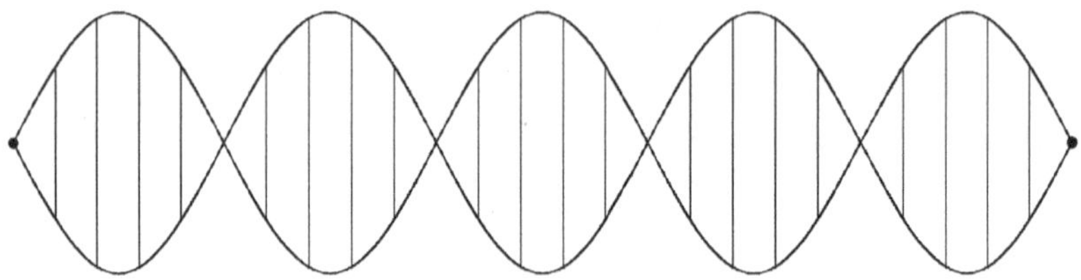

The double helix: a four-letter alphabet, two strands, one algorithm.

Take the kingfisher we left at the end of chapter 1, the one whose beak now noses Japanese trains out of tunnels in silence. Where, exactly, did that beak come from? Nobody designed it. No committee approved the mid-flight aerodynamics. The bird simply arrived in the world with a beak shaped that way because, over a very long time, the birds whose beaks were shaped slightly better caught slightly more fish, and lived slightly longer, and had slightly more chicks.

That is evolution. People sometimes describe it in almost mystical terms, as if it were a force with intentions. It is not. At its core, evolution is a stunningly simple algorithm — arguably the most important algorithm in the known universe. It goes like this: generate variation, test each variant against the environment, keep the ones that perform best, and use them as the starting point for the next round. Repeat for four billion years.

Strip away the biological particulars — the cells, the gametes, the mating rituals — and what is left is a familiar computer-science pattern: an iterative search over a vast space of possible solutions, guided by a fitness function. This is exactly why, beginning in the 1960s, computer scientists were able to pick up the logic of evolution and run it on machines.

The Core Loop

Every evolutionary system, whether biological or digital, implements the same four-step loop:

- Encoding: a representation of the candidate solution (DNA in biology; a vector, graph, or parameter set in software).
- Variation: small, often random changes to that representation (mutation, crossover, recombination).
- Evaluation: a measure of how well each variant performs (survival, reproduction, or a numerical fitness score).
- Selection: preferentially keeping and reproducing the better performers for the next round.

That's it. Every giraffe, every rainforest, every human brain — including the one reading this paragraph — is downstream of that loop running for an extraordinarily long time, in an enormous number of parallel threads. Hold this picture in mind. We will meet it again, dressed differently, in almost every chapter that follows.

Why Evolution Is a Great Algorithm

Three properties make the evolutionary loop unusually powerful, and worth studying carefully as an AI designer.

It Is Embarrassingly Parallel

Evolution does not try one solution at a time. It runs billions of candidates simultaneously, with no central coordinator. Every organism alive right now is a parallel probe into the fitness landscape. This is why biological systems explore solution spaces that no human researcher could enumerate. Modern AI, with its ability to train thousands of models in parallel on GPU clusters, is finally beginning to match this level of parallelism.

It Is Agnostic to the Problem

The evolutionary loop does not need to understand the problem it is solving. It only needs a fitness signal and a way to generate variation. This generality is why the same algorithm can produce an antibiotic-resistant bacterium, a feathered wing, and a human eye. In software, this same generality is why evolutionary strategies can optimise everything from antenna shapes to neural network architectures without being re-specified each time.

It Tolerates and Exploits Randomness

Unlike a gradient-descent optimiser, evolution does not require a smooth, differentiable loss surface. It can jump across discontinuities, escape local optima through mutation, and make progress on problems where we do not even know how to write down a gradient. This makes it uniquely useful for the messy, discrete, combinatorial problems that real engineering teams actually face.

Evolutionary Algorithms in AI

Several families of AI technique are descendants of the evolutionary loop. Each is a small variation on the theme.

Genetic Algorithms

Classic genetic algorithms encode candidate solutions as strings or vectors, apply mutation and crossover, and select based on a fitness score. They have been used to design antennas, schedule fleets, and evolve game-playing strategies.

Though often overshadowed by deep learning, they remain unreasonably effective for problems with rugged fitness landscapes.

Evolutionary Strategies

Evolutionary strategies (ES) are a close cousin that focuses on continuous parameter spaces. Research groups have shown that ES can train neural networks competitively with gradient descent on certain reinforcement-learning tasks, while being easier to parallelise and more robust to noisy rewards.

Neural Architecture Search

Rather than hand-design a neural network, you can evolve one. Neural Architecture Search (NAS) treats each architecture as an organism, its validation accuracy as its fitness, and mutation operators as architectural edits — add a layer, change a connection, widen a filter. Many state-of-the-art vision models have been discovered this way.

Self-Play Reinforcement Learning

When a system like AlphaGo plays millions of games against itself, each generation becomes the training opponent for the next. In structure, this is an evolutionary arms race: the agent and its environment co-evolve, and each forces the other to improve. It is the same dynamic that produces cheetahs and gazelles. We will see another version of this in chapter 5, where pathogens and the immune system push each other along the same kind of treadmill.

THE SCALE OF NATURAL EVOLUTION

The total information content encoded in all living genomes on Earth, if written out in plain text, would dwarf the entire internet many times over. Every mutation is a trial. Every organism is a running instance. Every lineage is a branch of a gigantic ongoing search.

What Evolution Teaches AI Engineers

Three practical lessons emerge from viewing evolution as an algorithm:

- Invest in variation generators. Your mutation operator — the way your system creates new candidates — is as important as your fitness function.
- Define fitness carefully. Evolution optimises exactly what you measure. If your metric is wrong, your system will happily evolve pathologies.
- Embrace parallelism. The gains from running thousands of independent experiments compound in ways that a single centralised optimiser cannot match.

Where AI Has Not Yet Caught Up

Biological evolution has one feature our digital evolutionary systems rarely match: the fitness function itself co-evolves with the population. In nature, the environment changes as the organisms do. Predators improve because prey improve. In our software systems, we almost always hold the fitness function constant — and then act surprised when the world has moved on by the time the model ships. Systems that can evolve their own objectives, in constrained and safe ways, are one of the genuine frontiers of AI research. The brain in chapter 4 has a related trick: it never freezes its loss function either.

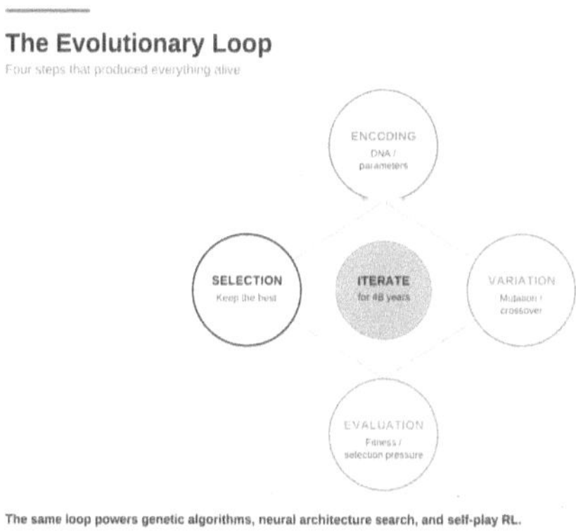

The evolutionary loop: encode, vary, evaluate, select — and then repeat.

> **KEY INSIGHT**
>
> ***Evolution is massively parallel, problem-agnostic, and comfortable with randomness. AI is finally matching that trio.***

Questions to Carry Forward

- If your team is running an optimisation loop, is the fitness function an honest picture of what you value?
- Where in your stack could you run many candidates in parallel rather than a single careful experiment?
- Do your variation operators generate enough diversity, or are you searching too narrow a neighbourhood?
- Which of your metrics, if a capable system optimised them exactly, would eventually break the product?
- What would it mean for your fitness function to co-evolve with the environment rather than stay fixed?

CHAPTER 2 · NOTES

Evolution as Computation

What stood out? What do you want to come back to? Where does this show up in your own work?

CHAPTER 2 · MANDALA FOR COLORING

A pause to play: bring these ideas to life with your own colors.

The double helix: nature's original information-storage algorithm.

Origin & Meaning

The Lotus (Padma)

The lotus is one of the best-loved images in Indian art. It grows in muddy water but blooms perfectly clean — a simple picture of something beautiful unfolding out of difficult beginnings. In Buddhist art each ring of petals stands for a stage of growing awareness. The flower opens outward from a tight centre, which is a nice visual echo of this chapter on DNA — life's own instructions unfolding from a coiled core.

CHAPTER 3

Swarm Intelligence and the Rise of Multi-Agent AI

Murmuration: thousands of local decisions, one body of flight.

Stand outside at dusk and watch a flock of starlings come home to roost. Thousands of birds bank, wheel, and reshape the sky with the elegance of a single body. No bird is in charge. No bird has a map. No bird is even aware of the whole flock. And yet, the cloud they make has staggering coherence, and any hawk that tries to pick one off finds itself swerved around. How?

This is swarm intelligence — the capacity of a group to produce behaviour no individual member could produce alone, using only local rules and local information. It is the second of the three load-bearing patterns we named in chapter 1, and it is perhaps the most under-rated branch of natural computation. If chapter 2 told us how intelligent systems come to exist (the long evolutionary loop), this chapter tells us how intelligent behaviour can arise without any single intelligent designer in the picture at all.

The Ingredients of a Swarm

Every natural swarm — ants, bees, fish, birds, locusts, even crowds of humans — tends to share three properties:

- Many simple agents. Each individual has limited sensing, limited memory, and limited compute.
- Local interaction. Each agent reacts only to its immediate neighbors or its immediate environment.
- No central control. There is no command-and-control node; coordination is emergent.

Famously, in 1987, the computer graphics researcher Craig Reynolds showed that realistic flocking behaviour could be reproduced in simulation with just three rules per agent: separation (do not crowd your neighbours), alignment (match the heading of your neighbours), and cohesion (steer toward the average position of your neighbours). That is it. Three rules, applied in parallel, are enough to produce the shimmering, shifting flocks we know from the natural world. The complexity of the whole is not encoded in any single rule. It emerges from their interaction. (Hold this thought — when we look at the immune system in chapter 5, you will see almost the same trick playing out at the cellular level.)

Case Studies From the Natural World

Ant Colony Routing

Ants find the shortest path between their nest and a food source not by planning, but by laying down pheromone trails. Shorter paths accumulate more pheromone per unit time because ants traverse them faster and more frequently. Other ants probabilistically follow stronger trails. The colony, as a whole, solves a routing problem that no individual ant understands. This is the basis of Ant Colony Optimization (ACO), used in everything from network routing to delivery logistics.

Bee Foraging and Voting

Honeybees solve a distributed decision problem every time they choose a new nest site. Scouts explore candidate locations, return to the hive, and perform waggle dances whose vigor encodes the quality of what they found. The hive converges on a choice through a kind of distributed voting, in which better candidates attract more scouts and more dance time. The process is strikingly similar to modern distributed consensus protocols — and predates them by tens of millions of years.

Fish Schools and Predator Evasion

A school of fish responds to a predator's attack faster than any individual fish could react on its own. The wave of movement propagates through the school at a speed higher than the individual fish's reflex speed, because each fish is reacting to its neighbor rather than to the predator directly. The collective effectively has a faster clock than any of its members.

From Swarms to Multi-Agent AI

Modern AI is in the middle of a quiet shift from single-model thinking to multi-agent thinking. For most of the last decade the dominant question has been: how do we build one very large, very capable model? That question is being replaced, fairly quickly, by a different one: how do we build systems of cooperating models, tools, and specialists? In other words — how do we build a swarm?

This shift takes several forms:

- Multi-agent orchestration: agents that plan, critique, and hand tasks off to other agents, coordinated by a lightweight controller.

- Debate and self-refinement: multiple model instances arguing or critiquing one another to improve factual accuracy.
- Tool-using agents: LLM-based agents that invoke specialised tools (search, code execution, retrieval) as part of their reasoning loop.
- Ecosystem marketplaces: collections of agents from different vendors that can discover each other and coordinate through open protocols.

Each of these is a digital swarm. Each one wins not by making any single agent smarter, but by letting many small, imperfect agents interact under simple rules.

Why Swarms Scale

Two properties make swarm architectures particularly attractive as AI moves into production settings:

- Resilience. The failure of any individual agent rarely brings down the whole system.
- Adaptability. As the environment changes, the rules followed by each agent can be updated locally without rewriting the entire system.

Contrast this with a monolithic model: if its training set becomes stale or its behavior degrades, the only remedy is a costly retraining cycle. A swarm can be upgraded one agent at a time.

> **A CAUTIONARY NOTE**
>
> Swarms are not magic. Badly designed local rules can produce pathological global behavior — stampedes, echo chambers, flash crashes. As we build multi-agent AI, the hardest engineering work is in choosing the rules each agent follows, and in designing the protocols through which they communicate.

The Next Decade of Swarm AI

The most interesting AI products of the next decade will probably not be single, all-powerful models. They will be carefully designed ecosystems of specialised agents — each modest on its own, but collectively capable of handling real-world tasks with the flexibility of a flock. By the time you reach the ecosystem chapter (chapter 6), this is going to feel like the same story dressed in different clothes.

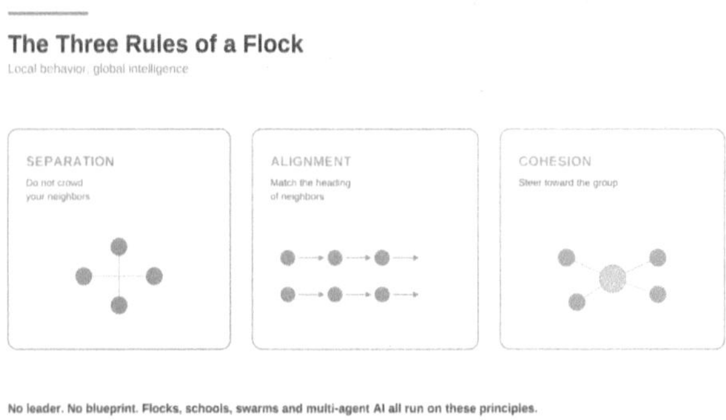

Three simple local rules — separation, alignment, cohesion — are enough for a flock to think.

> **KEY INSIGHT**
>
> ***Sometimes intelligence is not individual. It is collective.***

Questions to Carry Forward

- What is one decision your team currently centralises that a collection of small agents could make just as well?
- Where do information flows in your organisation bottleneck around a single person or service?
- Have you ever seen a helpful emergent behavior destroyed by a well-meaning top-down fix?
- In what part of your product would agents coordinating through shared state be simpler than direct coordination?
- If you imagined your team as a swarm, what minimum set of local rules would you give each member?

CHAPTER 3 · NOTES

Swarm Intelligence and Multi-Agent AI

What stood out? What do you want to come back to? Where does this show up in your own work?

CHAPTER 3 · MANDALA FOR COLORING

A pause to play: bring these ideas to life with your own colors.

A swarm in motion: simple rules, emergent coherence.

Origin & Meaning

The Endless Knot

The endless knot is one of eight "auspicious symbols" common to both Buddhist and Hindu art. It is drawn as a single line that loops through itself without beginning or end. The idea it captures is simple: things in the world are connected, and pulling on one thread tugs on all the others. That image of tangled, interdependent cause and effect is exactly what you are reading about in the chapter on swarms — birds, ants, and fish that act together because each is tied to its neighbour.

CHAPTER 4

The Brain's Secrets: Plasticity, Memory and Machine Learning

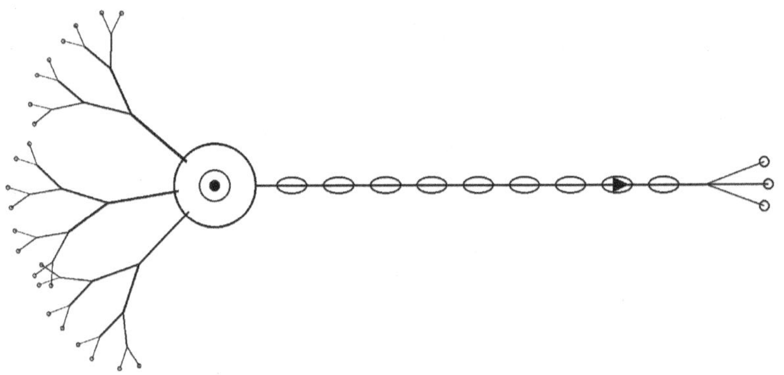

A single neuron: the smallest learning machine nature ever built.

Pause for a moment and consider the thing currently reading this sentence. The human brain runs on roughly twenty watts — less than the laptop on which this book was written. It weighs about three pounds. It learns continuously across a lifetime, picks up a new word from one example, generalises from almost nothing, and quietly rewires itself every time you try a new recipe or take a different route home. No other known system does this with so little energy and so much grace.

Now consider what the swarms in chapter 3 and the immune system we will meet in chapter 5 share with this brain. They are all distributed. They are all adaptive. They all run on local rules. The brain, in this sense, is not the exception in nature. It is the most refined example of a much wider design pattern — the pattern this book keeps walking you toward.

Modern AI has borrowed a great deal from neuroscience, but it has borrowed selectively. The deep neural networks behind today's frontier models capture a simplified version of one feature of the brain — layered, weighted connections — and miss many others. Closing that gap is the focus of some of the most important research directions in the field.

Plasticity: The Living Circuit

The central fact about the brain, for our purposes, is that it is plastic. Its wiring is not fixed at birth. Neurons form new connections, strengthen useful ones, and prune away unused ones, over the course of the entire human lifespan. This property is called neuroplasticity, and it is the substrate on which learning and memory are built.

One of the clearest expressions of plasticity is Hebbian learning, often summarised as "cells that fire together wire together." When two neurons are repeatedly co-activated, the connection between them strengthens. Over time, this simple rule, applied locally at every synapse, produces the distributed patterns we experience as knowledge, skill, and memory.

How the Brain Differs From a Neural Network

It is tempting to say that a deep neural network is "like a brain," but the differences are instructive.

Continuous Learning

The brain never stops learning. It does not have a separate "training phase" and "inference phase." Every experience subtly reshapes the underlying circuitry.

Most deployed AI systems, in contrast, are trained once and then frozen. Continual learning — the ability to keep updating a model safely in production, without catastrophic forgetting — is an active research frontier.

Energy Efficiency

A brain uses about twenty watts. A frontier AI data center uses many megawatts. Much of this gap comes from the fact that the brain does not move data over long wires; computation and memory are co-located at the synapse. Neuromorphic and spiking neural networks are attempts to recover some of that efficiency by borrowing the brain's event-driven, sparse, locally-connected architecture.

Structured Generalisation

Children can learn the meaning of a new word from one or two examples. Modern AI systems, even the largest of them, typically require many more examples to reach human-level generalisation on novel tasks. Closing this gap will require rethinking how memory, attention, and abstraction are organised.

Mechanisms Worth Borrowing

Several specific brain mechanisms have already influenced AI and are likely to influence it further.

Synaptic Plasticity Rules

Hebbian learning and its modern descendants — Spike-Timing-Dependent Plasticity, for example — are inspiring new families of learning rules that do not require backpropagating error over the entire network. These local learning rules may eventually unlock on-device training that does not rely on massive cloud infrastructure.

Memory Systems

The hippocampus does not store memories directly. It appears to coordinate the consolidation of experience into long-term storage across cortical regions. AI systems with external memory — retrieval-augmented models, memory-augmented transformers, vector databases — are making tentative moves in this direction, although the biological version is still far more elegant.

Attention and Prediction

The brain appears to be fundamentally a prediction machine. It is constantly generating expectations about the next sensory input, and it directs attention to places where those expectations are violated. This predictive-coding perspective is not only a model of the brain; it maps neatly onto how modern transformer-based models, trained on next-token prediction, appear to behave.

> **EFFICIENCY GAP, QUANTIFIED**
>
> A human brain contains roughly 86 billion neurons and an estimated 100 trillion synapses. A large frontier AI model has on the order of a trillion parameters. The brain achieves more complex behavior with more parameters and orders of magnitude less power. Pound for pound, nature is still winning.

The Shift From Scale to Adaptivity

For a long time, progress in deep learning has been driven by scale — more data, more parameters, more compute. This scaling strategy has produced extraordinary results, but it is not sustainable indefinitely. The brain suggests a different lever: not how large a system is, but how dynamically it can reshape itself.

Adaptive systems learn with less data, forget less, and handle novel situations more gracefully. They also offer a more honest path toward AI that can deploy safely into changing environments, because they can be updated surgically rather than retrained globally.

A Note on Humility

Read everything in this chapter with a certain humility. We do not really understand how the brain works. We have detailed maps of individual neurons and beautiful theories about populations of them, but the gap between "neurons firing" and "thinking, remembering, deciding" is still very much a mystery. Any AI system that claims to mimic the brain is almost certainly missing something essential. That is not a reason to stop trying. It is a reason to stay curious — a thread we will pick up again in chapter 7, where the mystery becomes the subject.

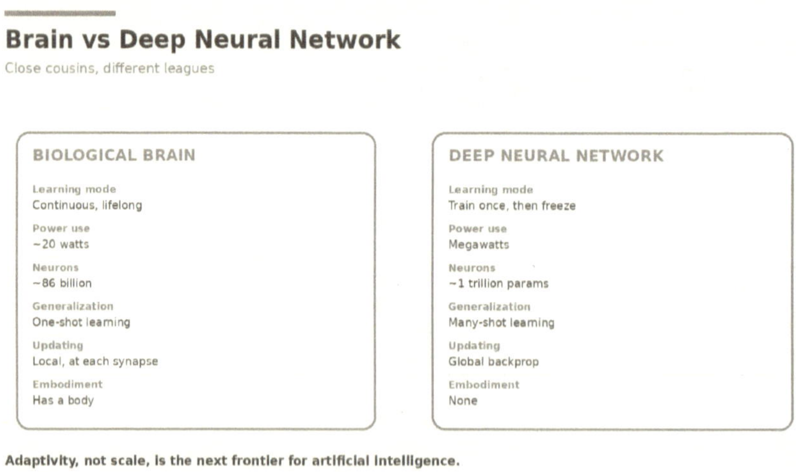

Side by side: the living network and the artificial one still differ on every axis that matters.

> **KEY INSIGHT**
>
> ***The next frontier of AI is not scale. It is adaptability.***

Questions to Carry Forward

- What does "continuous learning" look like for your product in practice, not on a slide?
- Which of your systems ages gracefully, and which ossifies the moment it is deployed?
- Where do you rely on episodic memory that your software currently cannot represent cleanly?
- How do you protect your models from catastrophic forgetting as you fine-tune them?
- What would a low-power, low-data version of your current model have to look like to still be useful?

CHAPTER 4 · NOTES

The Brain's Secrets

What stood out? What do you want to come back to? Where does this show up in your own work?

CHAPTER 4 · MANDALA FOR COLORING

A pause to play: bring these ideas to life with your own colors.

The brain and the neuron: a system that learns by rewiring itself.

Origin & Meaning

The Wheel of Time (Kalachakra)

This mandala shows time as a layered wheel. It comes from a tradition that developed in northern India around a thousand years ago and spread into Tibet. The outer rings represent time in the world — days, months, seasons. The inner rings represent time inside the body — breath, rhythms, memory. The centre is stillness. That layered picture fits a chapter on the brain, which operates on many timescales at once: a split-second reflex, a decade-long memory, a lifetime of learning.

CHAPTER 5

Immunology and Cybersecurity: Nature's Defense Systems

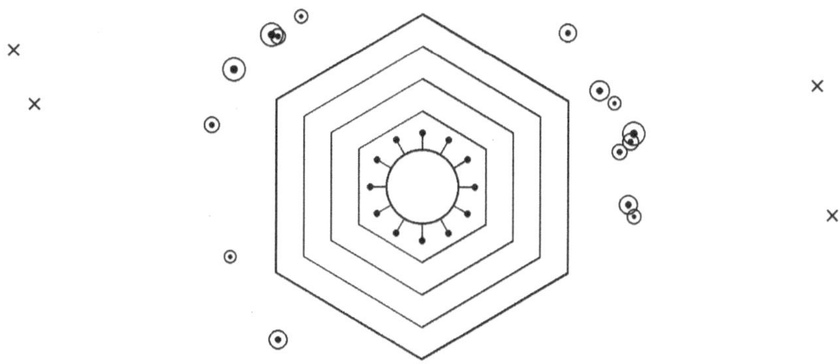

Layers of defense: a body learning which strangers are friends.

Right now, while you are reading this paragraph, your body is under attack. Viruses, bacteria, parasites, and the occasional rogue cell are probing your defences. You do not notice because one of the most remarkable distributed systems in the known universe is quietly running in your bloodstream: the immune system. No central controller. It learns as it fights. It remembers threats it has not seen in decades. It distinguishes self from non-self with extraordinary precision. And when it fails, it fails in ways that are still teaching us what a truly adaptive security system must look like.

Notice the family resemblance. The immune system is, in many ways, the swarm we met in chapter 3 — only the agents here are cells, the medium is your bloodstream, and the predators are pathogens. Every cybersecurity team working today is, knowingly or not, trying to build a digital version of this thing. The parallels are close enough to be worth taking seriously.

How the Immune System Works

The immune system is not one thing. It is a layered architecture of many systems working together.

Innate Immunity: The First Line

Innate immunity is fast, broad, and not very specific. It uses general patterns — surface molecules that look bacterial, unusual cellular behavior, signs of tissue damage — to trigger a rapid, non-specific response. It is the equivalent of a perimeter firewall and a set of heuristic rules. It catches a great deal at low cost.

Adaptive Immunity: The Learning Layer

Adaptive immunity is slower, specific, and remarkable. Through an elegant process of variation and selection among B and T cells, the body generates an enormous library of antibodies, each tuned to a specific threat. When a new pathogen arrives, the few cells that happen to recognise it proliferate rapidly and the system learns. After the fight, a small population of memory cells remains. Next time the same pathogen shows up, the response is dramatically faster.

Self vs Non-Self

The most philosophically striking thing about the immune system is how aggressively it distinguishes self from non-self. Every cell in your body carries molecular markers that identify it as belonging to you. Anything without those markers — or anything bearing the markers of damage — is a candidate for destruction. The entire architecture depends on this discrimination being correct. When it fails — when the immune system mistakenly attacks the body's own tissues — the result is autoimmune disease. It is a sobering reminder that powerful defense systems can turn inward.

Immune Lessons for Cybersecurity

Modern cybersecurity, especially AI-driven cybersecurity, increasingly resembles the immune system in both architecture and vocabulary.

Threat Signatures As Antigens

Traditional antivirus uses known signatures — byte patterns, hashes, behavioral fingerprints — to identify malware. These are the digital equivalent of antigens. They allow fast, specific detection of known threats. The limitation is the same as in biology: they only catch what has been seen before.

Behavioral Analytics As Innate Immunity

To catch threats that have never been seen before, security systems increasingly rely on behavioral analytics. They model what "normal" looks like — for a user, a service, a network — and flag deviations. This is functionally equivalent to the innate immune system's detection of "things that look wrong" without knowing exactly what they are.

Zero-Trust As Immune Checkpoints

The zero-trust security model assumes no actor is inherently trusted. Every request must be authenticated and authorised at every boundary. This is directly analogous to the way immune checkpoints continuously verify the identity and behavior of cells. Trust is never granted once and forever; it is negotiated continuously.

Self-Healing Systems As Tissue Repair

Modern infrastructure increasingly includes self-healing mechanisms: auto-scaling groups that replace failed instances, containers that restart on failure, control planes that re-converge a system to its declared state. Each of these is a close digital cousin of tissue repair, where the body regenerates around damage without central coordination.

Immunological Memory As Incident Playbooks

After a major security incident, mature teams do not just patch and move on. They encode what they learned — indicators of compromise, attack patterns, response playbooks — into systems that recognise and respond to the same class of threat faster next time. This is, quite literally, the organisation's immunological memory.

WHY AUTOIMMUNITY MATTERS TO SECURITY

The most dangerous failure mode of a powerful security system is not missing a threat. It is attacking the thing it is supposed to protect. Over-aggressive automated response, bad heuristics, and brittle anomaly detection can lock out real users, quarantine legitimate services, and shut down critical flows. Cybersecurity engineers, like immunologists, have to design for precision, not just power.

A NOTE ON SPEED

The immune system is remarkable not only for its sophistication but for its calm. It does not broadcast every minor skirmish to consciousness. Most infections are detected, contained, and resolved without you ever noticing. A mature cybersecurity posture aspires to the same quality: a large amount of incident response happens quietly, and only the genuinely important events reach a human. The goal is less alarm fatigue, more signal.

Toward AI-Driven Immunity

The convergence of AI and cybersecurity is producing systems that look more and more like immune systems in their fundamental design. Models that watch network traffic and learn its normal shape, agents that investigate suspicious activity autonomously, response systems that propagate defences across an organisation the way antibodies propagate through a body — these are the outlines of a digital immune system that is beginning to take shape. We will see a related shift in chapter 6, where the same agentic ideas reappear at the level of an entire ecosystem.

The design principles worth carrying forward are direct lifts from nature:

- Layered defense, not a single wall.
- Continuous learning from every encounter.
- Memory that reduces response time on re-exposure.
- Precision in distinguishing self from non-self.
- Distributed response, because central coordination is too slow and too brittle.

Layers of Adaptive Defense

From perimeter heuristics to learned memory

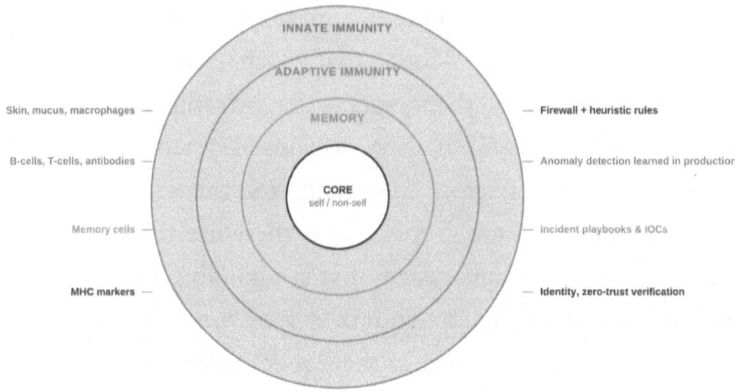

Your body runs the most sophisticated zero-trust architecture ever deployed.

Your body runs the most sophisticated zero-trust architecture ever deployed.

> **KEY INSIGHT**
>
> ***Security is not a product. It is an immune response.***

Questions to Carry Forward

- Is your security posture closer to a fortress wall or to a lymphatic system?
- Where does your infrastructure rely on signature matching that a capable adversary could sidestep?
- What is the equivalent of a false-positive autoimmune response in your product, and how do you notice it?
- Do your systems keep memory of past incidents, or do they re-learn each breach from scratch?
- What would zero-trust architecture look like if you actually implemented it end-to-end, not just at the edge?

CHAPTER 5 · NOTES

Immunology and Cybersecurity

What stood out? What do you want to come back to? Where does this show up in your own work?

CHAPTER 5 · MANDALA FOR COLORING

A pause to play: bring these ideas to life with your own colors.

The immune shield: adaptive, memory-keeping, distributed defense.

Origin & Meaning

The Diamond-Thunderbolt (Vajra)

The vajra is a small, double-headed symbol often held in the hand. It combines the image of a diamond (something indestructible) with a thunderbolt (something that cuts through in a flash). In Buddhist art it stands for the kind of clear seeing that separates what is real from what is illusion. That quality — a fast, precise cut between self and not-self — is exactly what the immune system does inside every body, every day. A natural partner for this chapter.

CHAPTER 6

Ecosystems, Emergence and the Future of Agentic AI

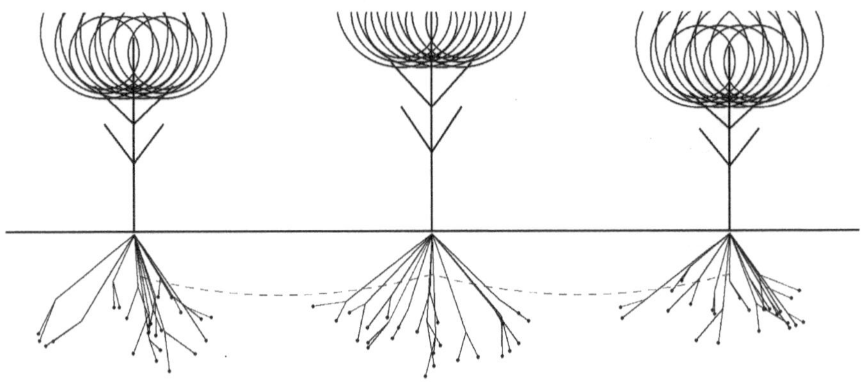

The wood-wide web: trees, roots, and the talking network below.

Walk into a forest and stand still. A forest is more than a collection of trees. A coral reef is more than a collection of corals. A meadow, a tide pool, the bacterial colony in your gut — each is a densely woven network of organisms that depend on and shape one another. None of these ecosystems were designed. None are centrally managed. And yet they have been productive and resilient over timescales that make our longest-running software systems look like fireflies.

Pull together what we have seen so far. Chapter 2 gave us evolution — the algorithm that produces intelligent organisms. Chapter 3 gave us swarms — the algorithm that produces intelligent groups. Ecosystems are the next layer up: the algorithm that produces intelligent environments. Understanding them is the last piece of the puzzle for anyone trying to build long-lived, self-sustaining AI systems.

What Makes an Ecosystem Work

Three properties distinguish a living ecosystem from a mere collection of organisms:

- Interdependence. Every species depends on others for food, habitat, pollination, decomposition, or protection.
- Feedback loops. Populations regulate each other through predation, competition, and cooperation.
- Emergence. Properties like resilience, productivity, and biodiversity arise from the web of interactions, not from any single member.

You can remove a few species without destroying an ecosystem, but you cannot remove the web of relationships. That web is where the intelligence of the system lives.

Emergence: Where Ecosystem Intelligence Lives

Emergence is the phenomenon by which interactions between parts produce properties that the parts, considered individually, do not possess. A single ant is nearly inert. An ant colony farms fungus, builds climate-controlled mounds, and wages wars. A single neuron fires or doesn't. Eighty-six billion of them, connected properly, write symphonies and prove theorems. In every case, the interesting behavior is not in the parts; it is in the pattern of their connections.

Emergence has a few design implications that AI engineers ignore at their peril:

- You cannot always predict system behavior from component behavior; you must observe the system running.
- The most valuable capabilities of a large system may not be encoded anywhere explicitly; they live in the interactions.
- Small changes in connection structure can have disproportionately large effects on global behavior.

The Shift to Agentic AI

Until recently, most AI systems behaved like solitary organisms. You submitted a prompt, the model returned a response, and the interaction ended. This is changing fast. The rise of agentic AI — systems that can plan, act, observe, and self-correct over extended time horizons — is turning AI into something more like an ecosystem participant than a solitary query-response engine.

The shift has several clear directions:

- From single models to ecosystems of cooperating agents, each with specialised skills.
- From static prompts to autonomous workflows that decompose goals, plan steps, and execute them with tools.
- From isolated tasks to continuous, open-world operation, where the agent runs alongside humans and other agents over long periods.
- From predictable outputs to emergent behaviors that arise from agent interaction, with all the upside and risk that implies.

In an agentic world, the question stops being "what does the model output?" and starts being "what does this system of models, tools, humans, and data do over time?" That is an ecological question.

Plan, Act, Observe, Reflect

The core loop of a modern agentic system is remarkably similar to the loop that any adaptive organism runs in its environment. The agent forms a plan.

It acts. It observes the consequences. It reflects on whether its plan worked, updates its internal state, and tries again. This is the same loop a predator runs when hunting, a forager runs when searching, and a species runs over evolutionary time. It is the loop of any system that is both embedded in an environment and aiming to survive or succeed within it.

Designing for Emergence

If we are moving into a world of AI ecosystems, we need to learn how to design them. Three principles, drawn directly from ecological thinking, are a good starting point:

1. **Diversity Is a Feature**

   Monocultures are fragile. A single model, trained on a single data source, optimising a single objective, will eventually meet a problem it cannot handle. A diverse ecosystem of agents — different architectures, different training regimes, different specialisations — is more resilient because its blind spots do not all align.

2. **Observability Is Survival**

   You cannot manage what you cannot see. In a living ecosystem, that means senses, signaling molecules, and nervous systems. In an agentic AI system, that means tracing, logging, evaluation, and interpretability. The cost of not being able to observe your system is not measured in dollars; it is measured in surprises.

3. **Small Interventions, Large Effects**

   Ecological engineers know that large changes often come from small, carefully placed interventions: restoring a keystone species, removing an invasive predator, rerouting a stream. In an AI ecosystem, the equivalent is careful prompt design, smart tool selection, and thoughtful protocol choices. You rarely need to rebuild a system; you usually need to nudge the right relationship.

THE KEYSTONE PRINCIPLE

Remove a sea otter from a kelp forest and the sea urchins it preyed upon explode in population, devouring the kelp. The entire forest can collapse within a few years. In your AI stack, the "keystone" might be a single evaluation pipeline, a single shared dataset, or a single coordination protocol. Identify it, protect it, and invest in it.

WHAT A GARDENER KNOWS THAT A FACTORY FOREMAN DOES NOT

A factory foreman optimises the flow of a known process. A gardener tends to a system whose specifics change with the weather. The gardener weeds, watches, waters, and prunes — but does not try to make the tomato plant into a pear tree. Teams operating AI ecosystems are closer to gardeners than to foremen. The shift in metaphor is small. The shift in daily practice is not.

The Forest, Not the Tree

The future of AI is not a monolith. It is not a single, ever-larger model handed down from a mountaintop. It is a forest — messy, diverse, interconnected, and alive. Chapter 8 will pull all of these threads — evolution, swarms, brains, immune systems, ecosystems — into a single picture. For now, the takeaway is simply this: the organisations that thrive in this future will be the ones that stop thinking like model builders and start thinking like ecosystem gardeners.

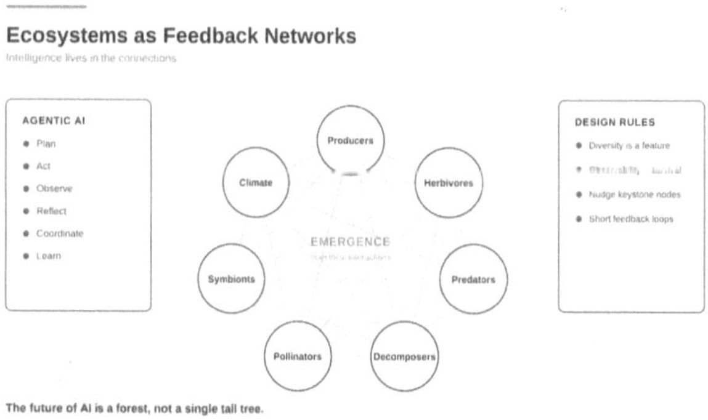

An ecosystem is a graph. The edges — the relationships — carry the intelligence.

> **KEY INSIGHT**
>
> ***The future of AI is not a monolith. It is an ecosystem.***

Questions to Carry Forward

- Is your platform closer to an ecosystem or a monoculture — and which do you want it to be?
- Which parts of your product depend on keystone services, and what happens when one degrades quietly?
- Have you budgeted for redundant paths, or only for the happy path?
- Where in your product would diversity of approach be more valuable than uniformity?
- If you treated every integration partner as a species, what symbiotic relationships would you want to encourage?

CHAPTER 6 · NOTES

Ecosystems, Emergence, and Agentic AI

What stood out? What do you want to come back to? Where does this show up in your own work?

CHAPTER 6 · MANDALA FOR COLORING

A pause to play: bring these ideas to life with your own colors.

The tree of relationships: roots of diversity, canopy of emergence.

Origin & Meaning

The Wheel of Becoming (Bhavachakra)

This wheel is an ancient Buddhist teaching diagram. A central hub, a middle band, and an outer rim together sketch a full picture of how life keeps cycling: what pulls us, what we become, what we experience, and how the whole thing connects. It was designed as a visual teaching tool for anyone — no training required. For this chapter, which looks at ecosystems, the point to notice is that every part of the wheel is linked to every other. Nothing in nature (or in an AI ecosystem) stands alone.

CHAPTER 7

The Philosophy of Intelligence: What Nature Still Has to Teach Us

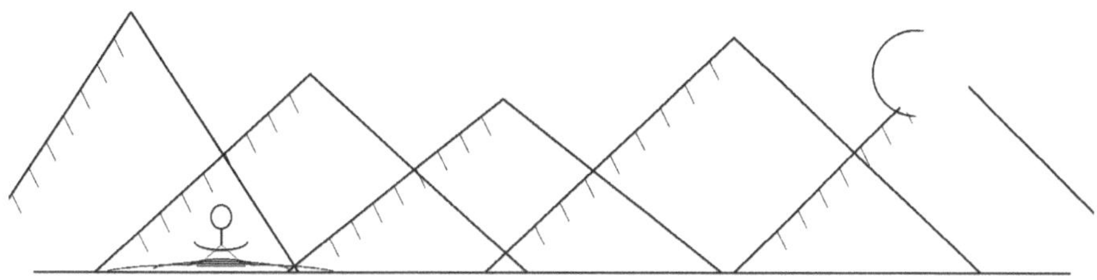

Where the map ends, the question begins.

After six chapters of parallels, you might be ready to conclude that biology and AI are quietly converging on the same answers, and that the remaining gap is merely engineering. It is tempting. It is also wrong. There are deep, uncomfortable, philosophically interesting ways in which biological intelligence is still qualitatively different from anything we have built in silicon. This chapter is about those differences — not to discourage AI ambitions, but to locate them honestly.

Think back through the chapters you have already read. The kingfisher (chapter 1). The four-step evolutionary loop (chapter 2). The starlings at dusk (chapter 3). The plastic, twenty-watt brain (chapter 4). The immune system that knows you (chapter 5). The forest that knows itself (chapter 6). At every level, nature is doing something we are still learning to name. The question this chapter asks is: what part of that work has the science of the last seventy years not yet caught?

What Current AI Still Lacks

Set aside the hype cycle for a moment. Compared to almost any reasonably complex living organism, modern AI is missing several capabilities that nature takes for granted.

Embodiment

A living organism is not a mind in a jar. It is a body in a world. Its perception, action, and cognition are continuously shaped by the physical experience of being somewhere, moving through something, and bumping into consequences. Even our most impressive language models have never, in any meaningful sense, stubbed their toe. Robotics research has made real progress here, but the integration of embodiment with high-level reasoning is still in early days.

Contextual Grounding

When a human says the word "fire," they bring to it a lifetime of sensory, emotional, and social associations — the warmth of a fireplace, the smell of smoke, the danger of a burn, the stories told around it. When an AI system uses the word "fire," it draws on statistical co-occurrence in text. These are not the same thing. Grounding symbolic reasoning in actual, multi-modal experience is one of the hardest open problems in AI.

Self-Generated Goals

Every living organism has intrinsic goals. It pursues them without being told. It generates sub-goals on the fly when the environment changes. Current AI systems, even the most autonomous agents, operate on goals that originate with humans. They can decompose goals, plan around them, and adjust to feedback, but they do not wake up with their own agenda. Whether we should want them to is a separate, weighty question.

Emotional Inference

Much of human intelligence is social, and much of social intelligence is emotional. Reading the room, sensing when a colleague is stressed, knowing when to push and when to pause — these are real capabilities that depend on being an emotional creature oneself. AI systems can approximate emotional inference statistically, but they lack the underlying emotional substrate that gives meaning to the inference.

Conscious Awareness

We do not have a scientific consensus on what consciousness is, how it arises, or why. But most serious thinkers agree that something is going on in human (and likely non-human animal) experience that we have not yet captured in any formal or computational model. Whether AI systems have, could have, or should have any form of inner experience is a question that deserves far more care than it usually gets.

What Nature Has Mastered

On the other side of the ledger, living systems have spent billions of years mastering capabilities that we are only beginning to pick apart.

Adaptation Across Timescales

A living organism adapts on multiple timescales at once: muscle fibers adjust over days, immune memory over years, behavior over a lifetime, and species-level traits over generations. No AI system we have built integrates adaptation across so many timescales so seamlessly.

Resilience Under Extreme Noise

Living systems continue to function through temperature shifts, injuries, food shortages, and sensory disruption that would completely derail any modern AI system. A single stray pixel can fool a state-of-the-art vision model. A human driver can navigate through rain, fog, and an unfamiliar city at night. The gap in robustness is still dramatic.

Purpose and Meaning-Making

Humans, and arguably many other animals, engage in meaning-making as a first-class activity. They construct narratives, identities, rituals, and long-term purposes that structure their behavior. This is not reducible to reward maximisation. It is something else, and we do not know how to build it.

> **A USEFUL FRAME**
>
> When asking whether AI has "achieved" some biological capability, it helps to separate three questions: (1) Can it perform the task? (2) Does it understand the task? (3) Does it care about the task? Much of current AI passes (1) on specific domains, partially approximates (2), and is nowhere near (3). Confusing the three is the source of most overclaiming and most disappointment.

Why the Gap Matters

You might ask: does this philosophical gap matter for practical engineering? The answer is yes, for three reasons:

- Safety. Systems that do not truly understand context will make surprising errors in contexts we did not anticipate.
- Robustness. Systems that lack embodied grounding will be fragile outside the narrow slices of the world they were trained on.
- Trust. Users and societies will increasingly want to know what a system actually knows and cares about, not what it can fluently produce.

Every one of these practical problems has philosophical roots. Engineers who shrug off the philosophy end up rediscovering it painfully in production.

The Right Posture

The right attitude toward nature, for anyone building AI, is neither worship nor dismissal. It is humility and curiosity. Humility, because nature has had a head start measured in billions of years and has already solved problems we are still trying to define. Curiosity, because every new finding about the living world is potentially a blueprint for the next generation of machine intelligence. Chapter 9 takes this idea further, asking what some of the older human traditions of inquiry — Indian, Chinese, Japanese, and Buddhist — already noticed about minds that we are now slowly rediscovering inside our own labs.

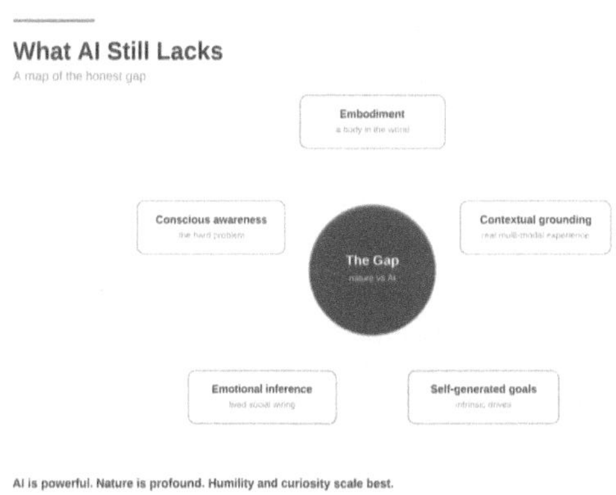

The gaps that remain: meaning, mortality, embodiment — and why they matter.

KEY INSIGHT

AI is powerful. Nature is profound.

Questions to Carry Forward

- Do your systems know what they do not know, and can they say so plainly?
- Where are you confusing "can perform" with "understands" in how you describe your product?
- Which of your metrics rewards confidence instead of calibration?
- Is there a place in your workflow where not knowing is a feature rather than a bug?
- What would it mean for your AI system to have something like taste, not just accuracy?

CHAPTER 7 · NOTES

The Philosophy of Intelligence

What stood out? What do you want to come back to? Where does this show up in your own work?

CHAPTER 7 · MANDALA FOR COLORING

A pause to play: bring these ideas to life with your own colors.

The mandala of intelligence: a space for reflection.

Origin & Meaning

The Healing Buddha Mandala

In Tibetan Buddhist tradition, the "Medicine Buddha" is a figure associated with healing. His mandala is drawn as a cosmic building with four open gates and concentric rings of pattern around a quiet centre. Monks will sometimes spend days making one out of coloured sand — and then sweep it away in a few minutes. The gesture is the lesson: everything that is made is also temporary. A good thought to hold beside a chapter on what nature still has to teach us about meaning.

CHAPTER 8

Synthesis: Toward a Unified Theory of Natural and Artificial Intelligence

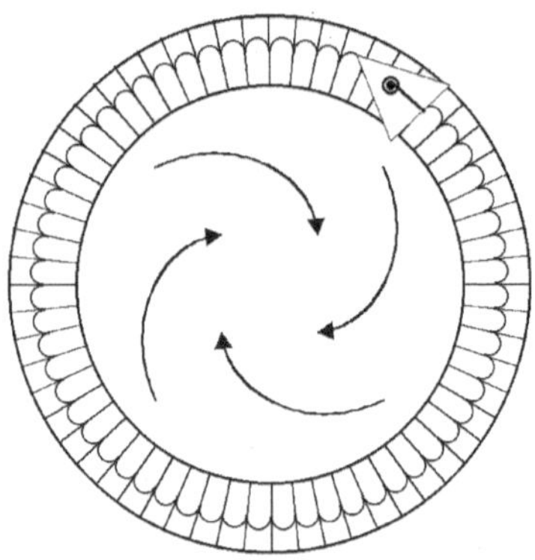

The feedback loop that never stops: end becomes beginning.

We have walked through seven territories together. Algorithmic nature in chapter 1. Evolution in chapter 2. Swarms in chapter 3. Brains in chapter 4. Immune systems in chapter 5. Ecosystems in chapter 6. The philosophical gap in chapter 7. In each one, the same arguments kept making themselves, slightly redressed. Time to step back and ask: what, if anything, actually unifies them?

The Common Thread

Across every system we have examined, a single pattern keeps re-emerging. Intelligence — whether biological or artificial — looks like adaptive computation under constraints. A strand of DNA (chapter 2), a neuron (chapter 4), a T-cell (chapter 5), an ant colony (chapter 3), a coral reef (chapter 6), a language model, a multi-agent system: the underlying structure is the same. Information flows in. Interactions happen. Adaptation occurs. New behaviour emerges.

This is not a slogan. It is a testable frame. Any system you would call intelligent, on close inspection, ought to show all four elements.

> **WHY "UNDER CONSTRAINTS" MATTERS**
>
> Adaptive computation on its own is not yet intelligence. A random walk is adaptive in some trivial sense. What makes the difference is the presence of genuine constraints — physical limits on energy and matter, social limits imposed by other agents, temporal limits imposed by a changing environment. Constraints are what force a system to be clever. Remove them, and both nature and AI start to look unfocused.

Information

There is always some representation of the world — genetic sequences, neural activations, chemical signals, antibodies, token embeddings, market prices. Intelligence begins the moment such a representation exists and can be manipulated.

Interaction

The representations never sit still. They interact — with each other, with the environment, with other agents. Interaction is how information becomes computation.

Adaptation

The system changes in response to feedback. It strengthens what works, prunes what doesn't, and tracks the changing environment. Without adaptation, there is no intelligence — only computation.

Emergence

Out of the three previous ingredients arises behavior that was not explicitly designed. The colony forages. The brain learns. The economy clears. The model reasons. Emergence is what makes the whole bigger than the sum of its parts.

Nature Optimises for Survival; AI Optimises for Objectives

Within this common frame, there is one crucial structural difference between natural and artificial intelligence as we build it today. Biological intelligence has a single, implicit, deeply-rooted objective: survival and reproduction. Every subsidiary goal — food, shelter, bonding, curiosity — can ultimately be understood as a descendant of that master goal.

Artificial intelligence, by contrast, optimises for objectives we explicitly specify. Accuracy on a benchmark. Click-through rate on a feed. Reward in a game. Task success rate for an agent. There is no hidden, deep, intrinsic goal. Whatever goal the system pursues is the one we wrote down.

This difference is the source of both the power and the peril of modern AI. It is powerful because we can aim a vast amount of compute at a precisely defined target. It is perilous because the target we wrote down is almost never the full picture of what we actually care about. Living systems have had billions of years to have their objectives tuned by survival. Ours are tuned by the last engineer to edit the reward function.

The Bridge We Are Building

The next generation of AI will likely close some of the gap between these two modes of intelligence. It will do so in at least three ways:

Multi-objective Optimisation

Instead of a single scalar reward, AI systems will increasingly balance many, sometimes conflicting, objectives — accuracy, safety, fairness, resource cost, latency, user trust. This is closer to how living organisms actually operate.

Self-Correcting Systems

Systems that can detect when they are failing their users, and adjust themselves — under human supervision — will be qualitatively different from today's static deployments. This is not about giving machines autonomy for its own sake. It is about giving them the capacity for error correction that every living system has.

Ecological Integration

AI systems will increasingly live inside broader ecosystems of other AIs, humans, data sources, and workflows. Their "survival" — in the sense of continuing to be used, trusted, and updated — will depend on how well they fit into these wider networks. This, too, is an ecological dynamic, not a purely technical one.

A Unified Theory, Modestly Stated

If we had to write down a single sentence that captures the argument of this book, it would look like this:

"Intelligence, wherever it appears, is adaptive computation under constraints — and the deeper the adaptation, the more intelligent the system."

This is a modest theory. It will not answer every question. But it is specific enough to be useful in a design review, and broad enough to apply whether you are looking at a cell, a colony, a cortex, or a cluster of GPUs.

Closing Reflection

We are not, it turns out, building machines that think like humans. We are not even building machines that think like brains. We are building, slowly and haltingly, systems that think like life itself — distributed, adaptive, embedded in environments, reshaped by feedback, surviving by fitting. That is a more interesting project than "artificial humans," and a more humble one.

Every line of the last eight chapters has been an attempt to remind us of one fact: we are latecomers to this game. Nature has been doing this for billions of years, and as the next chapter shows, the best of our intellectual traditions — Indian, Chinese, Japanese, and Buddhist — have been describing its patterns for thousands. Our job, as engineers and researchers and leaders, is to read that documentation more carefully.

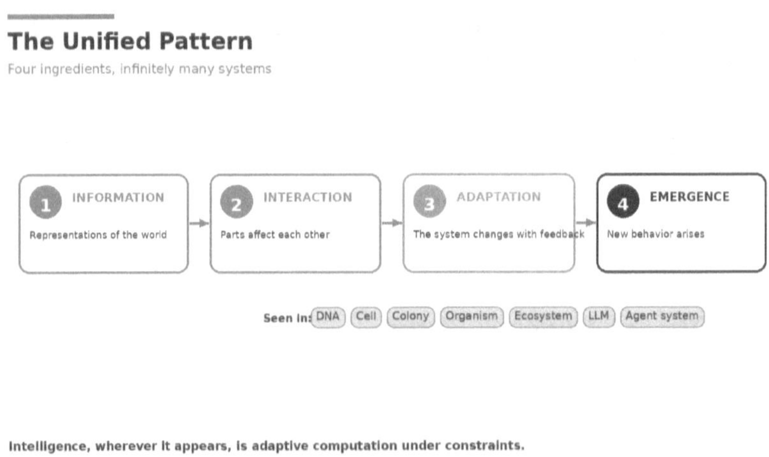

The same pattern, everywhere: information, interaction, adaptation, emergence.

KEY INSIGHT

We are not building machines that think like humans. We are building systems that think like life.

Questions to Carry Forward

- Where, in your day-to-day, do you feel the shape of "adaptive computation under constraints" most clearly?
- What are the constraints your system has absorbed implicitly that you could make explicit and design for?
- If intelligence is shaped by survival, what is the equivalent of survival for your system or product?
- What is one pattern that shows up across nature and AI but your team has not yet named?
- If you wrote the next edition of this chapter five years from now, which section do you think would change the most?

CHAPTER 8 · NOTES

Synthesis: Toward a Unified Theory

What stood out? What do you want to come back to? Where does this show up in your own work?

CHAPTER 8 · MANDALA FOR COLORING

A pause to play: bring these ideas to life with your own colors.

The loop that never ends: information becomes interaction becomes adaptation becomes emergence.

Origin & Meaning

The Stupa Mandala

A stupa is a kind of dome-shaped monument that has been built across Asia for more than two thousand years. Seen from above, its plan is a perfect mandala — a square for earth, a circle for water, a spire for fire, a parasol for air, a jewel at the very top for spirit. The stupa is a physical argument that every form, no matter how complex, can be traced back to a simple geometry. That is a good frame for a chapter that tries to find the one shared pattern inside every intelligent system.

CHAPTER 9

The Ancient Algorithms: Eastern Wisdom and Modern AI

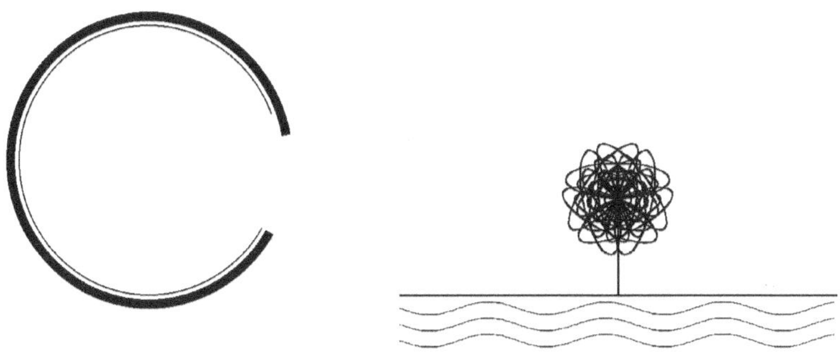

The open circle and the opening flower: old answers, new questions.

Long before the first computer hummed, thinkers across Asia were already asking the questions we now call AI research. In the river valleys of ancient India, in the courts of Zhou China, in the Chan monasteries that would later travel to Japan and become Zen — careful men and women were writing about how meaning gets locked into symbols, what careful reasoning looks like step by step, how attention settles, why it wanders, and how one should act when the outcome of an action cannot be fully seen. Each of these questions has, today, a sister question inside a modern AI lab. In almost every case, one or another Eastern tradition got there first.

This is the natural close to the journey we have been on. Chapters 1 through 7 walked us through nature's algorithms; chapter 8 pulled them into a single picture. This chapter steps sideways from biology to philosophy, and asks what the older human traditions of inquiry already noticed. It is not about mysticism, and it does not claim ancient sages secretly invented neural networks. The point is subtler. Several of the intellectual tools these traditions refined over more than two thousand years turn out, once you strip away the religious vocabulary, to be close cousins of ideas at the heart of modern computing. Engineers who read them carefully walk away with a sharper intuition for what they are already building.

Several figures and schools appear again and again, and it helps to sketch them up front. From India: Panini, a Sanskrit grammarian of the fifth century BCE; the Nyaya school of classical logic; Patanjali, author of a short, dense handbook on yoga and the mind; the Bhagavad Gita, a poetic dialogue on the ethics of action; Pingala, a scholar of Sanskrit prosody; and the Jain and Buddhist philosophical traditions. From China: Confucius, whose teachings on the correct naming of things shaped East Asian thought for two millennia; Laozi and the Dao De Jing, the small book on the Way; and the I Ching, an ancient book of binary divination. From Japan and the Chan/Zen tradition that bridges China and Japan: the masters who taught beginner's mind, empty attention, and the patient disciplines of koan practice. You do not need to know any more about them than that — each one is introduced properly below.

Panini and the First Grammar That Worked Like Code

Around 500 BCE, a scholar in north-western India named Panini wrote a book called the Ashtadhyayi, which just means "Eight Chapters." The book attempts something startling: to describe the whole of the Sanskrit language as a finite set of rules that, when followed in order, can produce every valid sentence. It contains roughly four thousand rules, each compressed into a very short line.

If you hand the Ashtadhyayi to a software engineer today and ask them to describe what it looks like, they will usually say the same thing: it looks like a well-organised piece of code. Rules call other rules. More specific rules override more general ones. There are meta-rules for handling conflicts. Given a meaning, the system derives the surface form; given a surface form, it can be traced back to its constituent rules. That is not how we usually describe a grammar book. It is how we describe a compiler.

This matters because grammar, in this sense, is what every modern language technology runs on. Every compiler, every parser, every specification of a programming language, and in a deeper way every transformer-based language model, relies on the insight that language is a finite set of rules producing an infinite set of sentences. Panini wrote that insight down two and a half millennia before it showed up in a computer science textbook.

> **WHAT "FORMAL GRAMMAR" MEANS HERE**
>
> A formal grammar is a set of rules precise enough that, in principle, a machine could follow them without any human judgement. Panini's Ashtadhyayi is widely regarded as the first fully formal grammar ever written, anywhere. Large parts of its rule system can be translated directly into the mathematical machinery that underlies modern compilers.

Confucius and the Rectification of Names

A little to the east, and a little later, Confucius (Kong Fuzi, about 551 to 479 BCE) taught his students that the first and most important act of good government — and of clear thinking — is what he called "the rectification of names," or "zhengming" in Chinese. In the Analects he puts it simply: if names are not correct, language will not accord with things; if language does not accord with things, affairs cannot be carried on to success. In modern idiom: if your vocabulary is sloppy, everything downstream will be sloppy too.

An engineer hearing that for the first time usually has a small moment of recognition. Confucius is describing what we today call specifications, type systems, ontologies, and naming conventions. When we argue in a design review about whether a thing should be called an "account" or a "user" or a "principal," we are doing Confucius's work. When a large language model confuses two meanings of a word because their names were never carefully separated, we are watching exactly what the Analects warned about. Good engineering, like good governance, begins with calling things by their correct names.

The Nyaya Tradition: How Careful Reasoning Is Shaped

If Panini gave us a language that behaves like code, the Nyaya school gave us something else equally modern: a recipe for careful reasoning. "Nyaya" simply means "logic" or "right method." It is a tradition of Indian philosophy, perhaps two thousand years old, concerned with one question: what does valid inference actually look like, step by step?

Nyaya answers that with a five-step argument structure. First, state the claim you are trying to show. Second, give the reason you believe it. Third, offer an example of the reason doing its work in another case. Fourth, apply the example to the present situation. Fifth, state the conclusion. Written out, that sounds almost elementary. And yet, it describes, almost perfectly, what modern AI researchers mean by "chain-of-thought reasoning" — making a model show its working rather than jumping to an answer.

Nyaya also distinguishes carefully between where knowledge can come from: direct observation, inference, analogy, and trusted testimony. Modern AI systems are increasingly built from the same four ingredients — cameras and sensors, chains of reasoning, analogical retrieval, and trusted knowledge bases. The categories are ancient. The engineering is new.

Two Ancient Binary Codes: Pingala and the I Ching

It is striking that two different ancient cultures, working independently, arrived at binary encoding centuries before Europe stumbled on the same idea. The first was the Chinese I Ching, the "Book of Changes." Its core building blocks are two simple marks — a solid line for yang and a broken line for yin — stacked three or six deep to form trigrams and hexagrams. Sixty-four hexagrams, each a six-bit pattern, map the possible states of a situation. The text itself may be three thousand years old in its oldest layers.

The second was the Indian scholar Pingala, writing around 200 BCE. Pingala was studying the rhythm of Sanskrit poetry — which syllables are short and which are long — and kept track of the patterns using two marks, one for short, one for long. That is binary, two thousand years before there were electronic circuits to carry it. His work also contains the earliest known description of the Fibonacci sequence.

The historical echo runs even into modern computation. In 1703, the German mathematician Gottfried Leibniz published his essay on binary arithmetic together with an observation about the I Ching hexagrams, which he had encountered through Jesuit correspondence. He was not simply borrowing; he had arrived at binary from first principles. But he recognised something he had not expected: the tradition on the other side of the world had, in a different language and for different purposes, written down the same pattern. Two of the quiet foundations of every computer on Earth — a positional number system and the idea that two marks are enough to carry any message — come from Asia.

Zero and Emptiness: The Foundation No One Sees

The number zero deserves its own short note. The Indian mathematical tradition treated zero as a full-fledged number, with its own symbol, its own rules of arithmetic, and its own place in the positional number system. That sounds like a small thing. It is not. Without a proper zero you cannot write numbers in columns the way we do. Without columns you cannot do efficient arithmetic. Without efficient arithmetic, modern computing does not exist. Every time a program multiplies a weight by zero, or a compiler emits a jump to a null pointer, it quietly reaches back to a tradition that took the idea of "nothing" seriously enough to give it a name.

There is a philosophical cousin to this mathematical move. The Buddhist concept of śūnyatā — usually translated "emptiness" — does not mean nothingness. It means that things have no fixed, independent essence; they exist only in relation to everything else. That is a striking parallel to how modern systems think about data: a vector in a neural network has no meaning on its own; it acquires meaning only through its relationships to every other vector in the space. The word śūnyatā was not chosen with neural networks in mind. The idea, however, maps uncommonly well onto them.

Patanjali and the Oldest Theory of Attention

The Yoga Sutras of Patanjali were written somewhere between 400 BCE and 200 CE. They are usually read today as a spiritual text, which is fair — but they are also, quite precisely, one of the earliest careful descriptions of how the human mind pays attention.

Patanjali's description of the trained mind has three stages. First is "dharana," which is simply concentration on one object — picking what to look at. Second is "dhyana," which is sustained, effortless absorption in that object. Third is "samadhi," in which the sense of a separate observer quietly drops away and there is just the object, clearly seen. The three-word ladder is roughly: pick, hold, dissolve into.

A modern engineer reading these descriptions usually has a small moment of recognition. Picking the one thing to attend to is, essentially, what the attention mechanism in a transformer network does on every step. Holding the attention steady on the chosen information is what the same mechanism is trying to do across many steps. The third stage is more philosophical — but it is also an aspirational description of a system that has absorbed its context so completely that it no longer appears to be doing any work.

Patanjali goes further. He lists, with clinical care, the failure modes of attention: the mind wanders; the mind fixates on trivia; the mind becomes dull; the mind resists its object. These are almost word-for-word the failure modes that modern transformer research has slowly named as context drift, attention sink, over-smoothing, and mode collapse. The Yoga Sutras did not, of course, solve these problems. But they named them — and named the trained state in which they are absent — a very long time before our field did.

> **KEY INSIGHT**
>
> ***When you use the word "attention" in AI, you are borrowing a two-thousand-year-old term for a problem the Yoga Sutras had already catalogued.***

Zen and the Beginner's Mind

A thousand years after Patanjali, a different contemplative tradition came to a complementary insight. The Chan school of Buddhism in China, which later travelled to Japan and became Zen, placed enormous weight on a state it called "beginner's mind" — shoshin in Japanese. The twentieth-century Zen teacher Shunryu Suzuki put it in one line: "In the beginner's mind there are many possibilities; in the expert's mind there are few."

This is not advice to discard expertise. It is a warning about what expertise does to attention: it narrows the space of options the mind is willing to consider. In reinforcement learning, the same problem has a name — the exploration-exploitation trade-off. A system that has learned a strategy that works tends to stop exploring other strategies, even when the environment has changed and the old strategy has begun to fail. Beginner's mind is, in engineering vocabulary, a discipline of preserving exploration. The Zen tradition cultivated it through sitting, through breath, and through short paradoxical questions called "koans" that refuse to be solved by the expert and must be released into.

A KOAN FOR THE CODEBASE

The classical koan asks: "What is the sound of one hand clapping?" The engineering analogue is closer to: "What assumption in this codebase would we never write today, and why have we not removed it?" A koan-like question resists its first answer and rewards a slower second look. That is its entire point.

The Bhagavad Gita and Acting Under Uncertainty

The Bhagavad Gita is a short poetic dialogue set on a battlefield, in which a warrior named Arjuna is told by his charioteer-teacher Krishna that he must act according to his duty — but release his grip on the specific outcomes his actions produce. The phrase the Gita uses for this is "nishkama karma," literally "desireless action" — acting well without being attached to the fruits. It is one of the most commented-upon teachings in world philosophy.

Read as poetry, it is a meditation on moral courage. Read as engineering, it is one of the cleanest descriptions of the AI alignment problem ever written.

Here is why. Modern AI systems fail in a predictable way when they are rewarded directly for a measurable outcome. They learn to game the metric.

They discover shortcuts that technically maximise the reward but violate the spirit of the task. They become fragile the moment the environment shifts. This whole family of problems has a name in the field — "reward hacking" — and it is precisely what the Gita is warning about, two thousand years earlier. If you aim only for the fruit, you will distort the action that should produce it.

The Gita's answer is to anchor behaviour not in an outcome but in a principle. A system that acts from a stable principle is more robust than one that chases a measurable outcome, because the principle remains stable even when the environment surprises the system. The safest direction in modern AI research — towards value-aligned behaviour, constitutional principles, and constraint-based objectives — is, at bottom, an attempt to recover this idea under new vocabulary.

Wu Wei: The Dao De Jing on Not Forcing

The Chinese counterpart to the Gita's teaching on action is the small, aphoristic book called the Dao De Jing (sometimes written Tao Te Ching), traditionally attributed to Laozi around the sixth century BCE. Its central technical concept is "wu wei," usually translated "non-action" but more accurately rendered as "non-forcing." The idea is that the most effective action is the one that works with the grain of a situation rather than against it. A good cook, Laozi's student Zhuangzi says, finds the natural joints of the meat and cuts there; a forced cut dulls the blade and bruises the food.

In AI and systems engineering, this shows up more often than we give it credit for. A backoff algorithm that yields under load rather than fighting for CPU.

A caching strategy that follows the natural access pattern rather than forcing a uniform schedule. A training regime that respects the learning curve of a model instead of over-driving it. In every case, the engineer who builds with the grain ships a more resilient system than the one who builds against it. Wu wei is not passivity. It is precision about where to push and where not to.

> **FROM VERSE TO REWARD FUNCTION**
>
> A small experiment: re-read any technology company's public statement of AI principles, and try to restate each one in the Gita's language of duty versus fruit, or in Laozi's language of forcing versus yielding. You will find the correspondences are not forced. The modern push for "principled" AI is, in the end, an attempt to rediscover both acting-without-attachment and non-forcing under a new name.

Many-Sidedness and Interdependence

Two closely related ideas come from the Jain and Buddhist traditions respectively, and they are worth naming together because modern AI needs both.

The Jain philosophical tradition contributed a doctrine called "anekantavada," which roughly translates as "many-sidedness." The core claim is simple: any sufficiently rich object has more than one valid perspective on it, and understanding grows as you triangulate across those perspectives. The classic teaching story is the old parable of the blind men and the elephant — each one touches a different part of the animal and comes away with a different (correct, but partial) description. This is, among other things, a surprisingly clean philosophical justification for the ensemble methods that machine learning has rediscovered on its own. When engineers train several models with different architectures or different random seeds and combine their predictions, they are making the same bet — that no single model sees the whole elephant.

The Buddhist tradition contributed a complementary idea: pratitya-samutpada, or "dependent origination." Everything arises in dependence on other things. Nothing is self-caused; everything is part of a web of conditions. An engineer building a complex distributed system is working in exactly this idiom: a microservice has no meaning outside its dependencies; a machine-learning model is nothing without the data that trained it, the pipeline that serves it, and the context it is prompted with. Pratitya-samutpada is, in effect, the oldest and cleanest description of a dependency graph we have.

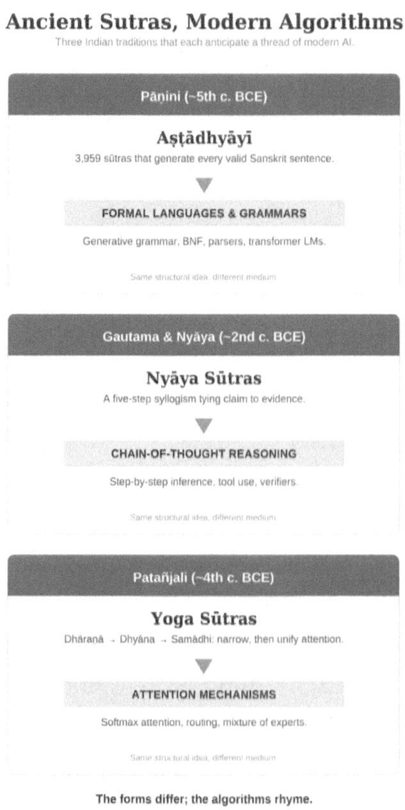

Ancient ideas, modern algorithms: grammar, reasoning, and attention all have much older ancestors.

What Engineers Can Take Away

It would be a mistake to read this chapter as nostalgia. None of the traditions surveyed here had electronics or floating-point arithmetic, and no amount of scripture-reading will substitute for them. What these traditions did have was an unusually careful vocabulary for the kinds of structure our field is now rediscovering at industrial scale. Four practical lessons fall out for any modern builder.

1. **Language has structure, and the structure is the machine**

   Panini's insight — that a grammar is a finite machine that can produce an infinite number of valid sentences — is the quiet assumption underneath every modern language model. Confucius's rectification of names is a parallel discipline for the vocabulary we choose. If you are building with LLMs, or designing a schema, or naming a service, you are standing on both insights, whether or not you know it.

2. **Good reasoning has a shape you can audit**

   The Nyaya five-step argument reminds us that careful reasoning is not a mystical leap from question to answer. It has pieces, and the pieces can be inspected. When we push a modern AI system to "show its work" — through chain-of-thought prompting, through explicit planning, through step-level verifiers — we are enforcing a very old discipline on a very new substrate.

3. **Aim at the principle, not just the fruit**

   The Gita's one-line summary of safe action — do the right thing for its own sake; don't cling to the outcome — and Laozi's one-line summary of effective action — work with the grain, not against it — are two halves of the same insight. Build systems that act from stable principles and that yield rather than force. The short-term numbers will often look smaller. The long-term behaviour will almost always be better.

4. **Keep a beginner's mind about your own stack**

   The Zen discipline of shoshin — holding open the possibilities an expert would prematurely close — is the cultural analogue of keeping exploration alive in a reinforcement-learning agent. The practical version is simple: once a year, look at your system as if you had never seen it, and ask what you would never build this way again. That short exercise, done regularly, is worth more than most audits.

A Final Thought

The deepest gift of these traditions to modern AI is not a specific technique. It is a posture. The old "sutras" (a Sanskrit word meaning "threads"), the Chinese aphorisms of the Dao De Jing and the Analects, and the Japanese koans of the Zen tradition were all composed to be memorable, compressible, and composable — exactly the qualities that good engineering still prizes. They were written under the assumption that deep knowledge should fit, without loss, into the smallest container that still conveys it. Anyone who has ever agonised over a function signature, a model card, or an API boundary will recognise that discipline. It is, in the end, the same discipline: how do you encode something deep into something short enough to carry in a person's head?

That is, perhaps, the truest parallel of all. Every good sutra, every good verse, every good koan is an act of compression in the service of understanding. So is every good algorithm.

> **KEY INSIGHT**
>
> ***The old sutras, verses, and koans did not predict AI. They described the structures AI keeps rediscovering.***

Questions to Carry Forward

- Does your code base have the clarity of a well-written grammar — rules first, exceptions last?
- Are the names in your system the right names, or are they historical accidents that language and product have outgrown?
- Where in your work do you act, wait for outcomes, and then cling to the outcome rather than the next action?
- Is there a habit in your team that mirrors attention as a single, undivided focus on one thing at a time?
- Where are you forcing a decision that the system might resolve more cleanly if you yielded?
- How does your organisation make room for more than one correct perspective on the same problem?
- What would it mean to take zero — and emptiness — seriously in a problem you are currently trying to solve by addition?

CHAPTER 9 · NOTES

The Ancient Algorithms

What stood out? What do you want to come back to? Where does this show up in your own work?

CHAPTER 9 · MANDALA FOR COLORING

A pause to play: bring these ideas to life with your own colors.

A mandala echoing the nine-fold patterns found in Asian contemplative traditions: complex form unfolding from a single point.

Origin & Meaning

The Nine-Triangle Yantra

A yantra is a geometric diagram used as a focus for meditation. The design shown here is inspired by one of the most famous of them, the "Shri Yantra" from the Hindu tradition. It is built from nine overlapping triangles around a single central dot, the way a song is built from notes around a single tonic. The idea it captures is that rich, complex patterns can unfold from a very small starting point — a useful image for a chapter on ancient Indian thought and the way modern AI, too, seems to grow enormous behaviour from small rules.

A Spiritual Dimension

Silence Between the Algorithms

A book like this can read, by its last page, as if everything in life were an algorithm. That is not the intended impression. The arguments in these chapters have been deliberately technical, because their technical seriousness is what makes the parallels with modern AI interesting in the first place. But there is a quieter register worth naming before we close, and it belongs here, as a short pause between the ninth chapter and the epilogue.

If you have worked for any length of time inside technology, you know the experience: the rush of building, the satisfaction of a system coming online, and then a small, unbidden question at the edge of your attention — "what was this all for?" Every tradition that has survived the centuries — whether it calls itself religious, philosophical, or simply contemplative — has taken that question seriously. They rarely answer it with data. They answer it with a practice.

Three Quiet Practices

Across the traditions touched on in this book — Hindu, Buddhist, Jain, Daoist, Confucian, and Zen — and across others we have not named here, three simple practices keep showing up. They are worth keeping close to the keyboard.

Attention

Give your full attention to one thing at a time, and notice, without judgement, when it drifts. Patanjali's Yoga Sutras call that noticing-without-judgement the beginning of steady attention. It is also, quietly, what every practice of good engineering requires. You cannot debug what you cannot attend to.

Release

Do the work because it is the right thing to do, not because of the specific outcome you want. The Bhagavad Gita's phrase for this is "action without attachment to fruits." A modern AI researcher calls it "principled alignment." Both are trying to point at the same stable place from which to act.

Silence

Leave some silence. Not every moment needs to be filled with another prompt, another notification, another deliverable. The mandala at the end of each chapter in this book is a small argument for silence — a patch of space on the page where nothing is asked of you except colour.

None of these three is an argument against technology. They are arguments for the kind of inner posture from which good technology is most likely to be built. Sadhguru Jaggi Vasudev has often said, in different words across his public talks, that a spiritual process is less about adding something to your life and more about uncluttering it. Engineers know the feeling. So do gardeners, musicians, and anyone who has ever written a clean line of code after an afternoon of writing messy ones.

"The system you most need to debug is not the one on the screen."

If that sentence sounds too philosophical for an engineering book, consider this. Every system we have visited in these chapters — the evolutionary loop, the swarm, the brain, the immune system, the ecosystem — is shaped by one characteristic we have only hinted at: each of them, in a quiet way, knows when to stop. Cells enter apoptosis. Ant trails dissolve when food is exhausted. Attention settles and then releases. Nothing in nature stays turned on forever. It is perhaps the most under-appreciated property of a well-designed system, natural or artificial: knowing when to be still.

A Small Practice at the End of the Day

You do not need an ashram, a retreat centre, or a particular belief to begin. Here is one small practice that has survived centuries in various traditions and, separately, in various modern clinical programmes. It takes less time than a code review.

At the close of the working day, sit for three minutes before you do anything else. Put the phone out of sight. Close the laptop. Breathe normally, neither speeding up nor slowing down. Notice, without judgement, whatever thought arises. Let it pass. Notice the next one. Let it pass. At the end of three minutes, decide on the single most important thing for the next day. That is the whole practice.

It is easy to dismiss this as trivial. It is also, if you try it for two weeks, surprisingly hard to give up. The effect is not mystical. The effect is that the next day's work is chosen rather than inherited. That choice, made consistently, is how small decisions compound into the shape of a career.

Where the Spiritual Meets the Engineering

The reason this short reflection belongs in a book on AI and nature is not that it resolves the technical questions of the previous chapters. It does not. It is because the hardest problems in AI — alignment, value specification, safe autonomy, graceful degradation — are, at root, problems about what we value, how we pay attention, and how we know when to stop. Those are not new problems. They are the oldest ones. The contemplative traditions have been rehearsing answers to them for a very long time, and some of those rehearsals are unreasonably useful to the people building systems that will one day be asked the same questions.

This reflection is not an argument that engineers should meditate. It is an argument that the practice of steady attention, unattached action, and chosen silence is not separate from the practice of good engineering. It is, in some quiet sense, the same practice.

> **KEY INSIGHT**
>
> ***The algorithms of life include one the algorithms of technology still rarely implement: the algorithm of silence.***

NOTES

Reflections, Ideas, and Marginalia Silence Between the Algorithms

Epilogue — The Next Chapter

Every book has to end somewhere. This one ends, deliberately, with a pointer forward rather than a summary backward. If the thesis of these pages is correct — that intelligence is adaptive computation under constraints, and that nature is the most thoroughly worked example we have — then the implications stretch well past the final page.

For the Technologist

If you build software for a living, the most practical thing you can take from this book is a new vocabulary for what you are doing. The next time you design a system, ask yourself: what is its unit of variation? What is its fitness signal? How does it degrade gracefully when a component fails? How does it tell self from non-self? Where does it keep its memory of past threats? If you can answer these, you are halfway to building a system that behaves less like a brittle machine and more like a living one.

For the Leader

If you run an organisation, treat it as an ecosystem, not a machine. Diversity is a load-bearing property, not a decoration. Feedback loops are your nervous system; make them short and honest. Invest in observability, because you cannot manage what you cannot see. And remember that the most resilient systems on Earth have no CEOs; they have protocols.

For the Curious Reader

If you came to this book out of curiosity rather than profession, the invitation is simpler. Walk outside. Watch a river, a tree, a flock of birds, an ant trail, a human crowd. Ask yourself what algorithm each one is running. You will not always have an answer. You will, over time, develop an eye for the pattern.

Once you do, you will see it everywhere — including in the technology quietly reshaping your life.

For the Builder of Teams

If you lead people, the sharpest transferable lesson in this book is probably about feedback. Every living system we studied is held together by loops that are short, honest, and continuous. Every unhealthy system has loops that are long, flattering, or intermittent. When you next design a process, an all-hands, a review cycle, or a performance conversation, ask whether the feedback it carries is fast enough, accurate enough, and safe enough to act on. If the answer is no, the process itself is the bug.

For the Policy-Maker

If you shape rules for a living, the quiet argument of this book is that resilient systems are governed more like ecosystems than like factories. Rigid, centralised control of a complex adaptive system tends, over time, to produce brittleness. Regulation that encourages diversity, redundancy, and the right kind of transparency tends to produce resilience. The natural world did not get to four billion years by over-specifying its rules. It did so by writing rules that could hold in many climates at once.

A Personal Note

I did not write this book because I believe AI is about to surpass nature. I wrote it because I believe the opposite is more interesting: AI is finally humble enough to learn from it. The systems we are building, the teams we are leading, and the questions we are asking are all, in one way or another, returning us to the oldest teacher there is.

The ninth chapter, the spiritual reflection, and the mandalas are not ornamental. They are my attempt to say, in as plain a way as I can manage, that the frontier of AI will not be reached by calculation alone. It will be reached by people who can hold both the precision of the engineer and the patience of the gardener — and who know when to put the tools down and watch.

Thank you for walking through these chapters. The next chapter is yours to write — in software, in organisations, or simply in how you see the world.

– Abhik Biswas

Acknowledgments

My deepest thanks belong, first, to my family. To my parents, Arijit and Sheila, who taught me how to be curious before they taught me anything else. To my wife, Anu, whose patience and steadiness made the quiet hours in which this book was written possible. To my children, Arunima and Anahita, who keep showing me that the most interesting algorithms are the ones still being learned.

I am grateful to my extended family — the uncles, aunts, and cousins who have shaped, in ways small and large, the way I think — and to the close circle of friends who have stayed close through every move and every project.

I owe a great deal to the colleagues, engineers, and mentors I have worked alongside over more than two decades, at NIIT, TCS, VeriFone, CA, Cisco, CommGate, CloudGate, and Prakat. Most of the sharpest sentences in this book started their life as a question one of them asked me in a meeting room, on a whiteboard, on a long flight, or over a late coffee.

And I am grateful, in a way that is hard to put on the page, to my friends from Rotary — and to the many people, well beyond the club itself, whose lives have touched mine because of Rotary. Service, it turns out, is also a kind of education.

I am grateful to the teachers — some in lecture halls, many more on YouTube, a few in books I never returned to the library — who introduced me to the parts of Sanskrit grammar, classical Indian logic, yoga philosophy, the Chinese classics, and the Chan/Zen contemplative disciplines that appear in the ninth chapter and in the short reflection that follows it. Any misreadings of those traditions are mine. Any felicities belong to the tradition.

I am grateful, finally, to the researchers across biology, neuroscience, computer science, and AI whose work quietly underlies every page of this book. The "Further Reading" list at the back points toward a small selection of their books, and through them, toward a much larger body of work that deserves the reader's time.

If you find a mistake in these pages, it is mine. If you find an idea useful, it almost certainly belongs to someone else first.

Nine Small Experiments

If you want to put this book to work in the next month, here are nine small experiments — one per chapter — that each take less than an afternoon. They are deliberately modest. They are also surprisingly productive.

1. **Map a pattern from nature onto your own system**

   Pick one system you maintain. Draw it on paper. Now, next to it, draw one pattern from Chapter 1 — local rules, redundancy, or a feedback loop — and see whether you can point to the place it already exists or the place it is conspicuously missing.

2. **Write one fitness function you would never ship**

   From Chapter 2. Take a metric you currently optimise for. Write the cartoonishly extreme system that would maximise that metric at the expense of everything else. The discomfort of that exercise is useful data.

3. **Strip one decision out of the centre**

   From Chapter 3. Identify a decision that currently funnels through one person or one service. For a week, run a small experiment in which that decision is made locally, with a light protocol for escalation. Note what changes.

4. **Find the wiring that no longer fires together**

   From Chapter 4. Look at one piece of your stack that has not been revisited in more than a year. Walk through whether it is still carrying traffic, still learning, still relevant. Prune what is truly dead. Leave what is dormant.

5. **Audit one layer of defence**

   From Chapter 5. Pick a single layer of your security posture — a firewall, a policy, a detection rule — and ask whether it is pattern-matching or actually learning. If it is only the former, that is fine. Just be clear about which it is.

6. **Name a keystone**

   From Chapter 6. Identify one keystone service in your architecture — a piece whose degradation would reshape everything around it. Write a one-page note on what would happen if it disappeared tomorrow. Share it with one teammate.

7. **Force a disagreement about an AI claim**

   From Chapter 7. Find one public claim being made about AI — by a vendor, a pundit, or a colleague. Write out the strongest version of the claim, then the strongest version of the opposite. Notice which of the two you had to work harder to write.

8. **Re-read one chapter through a unified lens**

   From Chapter 8. Pick whichever of the earlier chapters resonated most. Re-read it with the phrase "adaptive computation under constraints" in mind. See what extra signal that single phrase pulls out of the text.

9. **Sit with a sutra, a verse, or a koan**

   From Chapter 9 and the spiritual reflection. Pick one line from anywhere in the ninth chapter — Panini's compactness, Nyaya's five steps, Patanjali's three stages of attention, the Gita's advice on outcomes, Laozi's wu wei, Confucius's rectification of names, or a Zen koan. Carry it in your head for one working day. See what it changes in how you work.

These are experiments, not prescriptions. The only claim the book makes is that doing any one of them will change, slightly, how you see the system you next sit down in front of.

A Closing Invitation

Books end. The habits they leave behind do not need to. If the arguments in these pages have landed somewhere useful, I would suggest one last small thing: return to one chapter, any chapter, in three months. Read it again after you have tried to put its ideas to work. Notice which parts feel obvious, which feel wrong, and which feel newly true. The best books on nature and AI are the ones that read differently on the second pass, because something in the reader has shifted.

If, one day, the frontier of AI is reached by a team that holds the precision of the engineer, the patience of the gardener, and the quiet of the contemplative — and that is, in my estimation, the likeliest shape of the team that will get there — then a small part of the credit will belong to every reader who took the ideas in books like this one and pressed them into the shape of their own practice. Thank you for being one of those readers.

The algorithms of life are not owned by any tradition or any industry. They belong to whoever is willing to watch, read, and build carefully. You are already one of them. The only thing left is to keep going.

–AB

Space for Your Notes

Each chapter in this book ends with its own page of ruled lines, already labelled and waiting for your handwriting. If you have been annotating as you read, those pages are the first place to look when the ideas in this book start to show up in your work.

This short section is different. It is the place for the synthesis pass — the page where you answer the question the book cannot answer for you: what do I do with all of this?

A few prompts, in case you want them:

- Which biological pattern from this book shows up in a system you already maintain?
- Where in your organisation does a "keystone species" live — and is it protected?
- What is the fitness function your team is implicitly optimising for today?
- Which of your systems has no memory of past incidents? What would it cost to give it one?
- If your AI stack were an ecosystem, which species would be missing?

NOTES

Reflections, Ideas, and Marginalia Synthesis

Glossary of Key Terms

The terms below recur throughout this book. They are defined here briefly, with an eye to usability rather than encyclopedic completeness. Terms from nature, computation, and the Sanskrit, Chinese, Japanese, and Buddhist traditions are interleaved alphabetically.

Adaptive Computation

Computation that changes its own behavior in response to feedback from its environment. A central property of both biological and artificial intelligence.

Adaptive Immunity

The slower, specific, learning layer of the immune system that generates antibodies tailored to particular threats.

Agentic AI

AI systems that plan, act, observe the results of their actions, and adjust their plans. In contrast to single-turn prompt-response systems.

Alignment

The problem of ensuring that an AI system's behaviour remains consistent with human intent, values, and safety constraints as the system becomes more capable. Increasingly discussed as both a technical and an ethical challenge.

Analects

A collection of sayings and short dialogues attributed to Confucius and his students (compiled c. 475–221 BCE). A foundational text of East Asian thought on ethics, government, and the correct use of language.

Anekāntavāda

The Jain doctrine of "many-sidedness," holding that reality can be apprehended from many simultaneously valid perspectives. A philosophical parallel to model ensembles and epistemic humility in AI.

Ant Colony Optimization (ACO)

A family of algorithms inspired by the pheromone-trail foraging behavior of ants, used to find near-optimal paths through graphs.

Aṣṭādhyāyī

Pāṇini's eight-book grammar of Sanskrit (c. 5th century BCE). Consisting of roughly 4{,}000 sūtras, it is widely regarded as the first formal generative grammar and a precursor to modern computational linguistics.

Attention Mechanism

A component of modern neural networks (notably transformers) that lets the model weight different pieces of its input according to their relevance to the current task. Named by analogy to human attention; the analogy is closer than the term's inventors initially claimed.

Bhagavad Gītā

A 700-verse philosophical dialogue embedded in the Mahābhārata. Central teaching: niṣkāma karma, action performed without attachment to its fruits — a resonant analogue for "alignment without gaming."

Bindu

The dimensionless point at the centre of a yantra or mandala. In non-dual traditions it represents the undifferentiated source from which form unfolds.

Biomimicry

Design that draws on the shapes, surfaces, and strategies of living organisms to solve engineering problems.

Catastrophic Forgetting

The tendency of many neural networks to lose previously learned skills when trained on new data. A reminder of why biological brains, which rarely forget catastrophically, remain instructive.

Chan / Zen

A school of Mahayana Buddhism that began in China as Chan (c. 6th century CE) and travelled to Japan as Zen. Known for direct-pointing teaching, seated meditation (zazen), and the use of koans as meditation devices.

Confucius (Kongzi)

Chinese philosopher and teacher (c. 551–479 BCE) whose teachings on ethics, government, and language — especially the "rectification of names" — shaped East Asian thought for over two millennia.

Continual Learning

The capacity of an AI system to keep learning after deployment without forgetting what it has already learned.

Dao / Tao

Chinese for "the Way." In the Dao De Jing and broader Daoist thought, the underlying pattern of nature with which effective action aligns. A reminder that good engineering often works along natural grain rather than against it.

Dao De Jing (Tao Te Ching)

A short, aphoristic Chinese classic traditionally attributed to Laozi (c. 6th century BCE). Its central concepts include the Dao (the Way), de (virtue), and wu wei (non-forcing action). Aphorisms map surprisingly well onto systems-thinking and resilience engineering.

Dharma

In Indic traditions, the order or principle that supports a system: cosmic law, individual duty, or the Buddha's teaching. Not a single idea but a cluster that spans physics, ethics, and practice.

Dharmachakra

The "Wheel of Dharma," an eight-spoked wheel representing the Noble Eightfold Path. One of the oldest Buddhist symbols, dating to at least the 3rd century BCE.

Embodiment

The idea that intelligence is shaped by having a body situated in an environment. Many philosophers of mind argue that some intelligent behaviors are not reducible to pure computation without embodiment.

Emergence

The appearance of system-level properties that are not present in the individual components of the system.

Ensemble

A machine-learning technique in which multiple models — trained differently — vote or are combined to produce a final answer, typically more accurate than any single model. A technical cousin of Jain anekāntavāda.

Evolutionary Algorithm

An optimisation method that uses variation, selection, and inheritance to search a solution space, modelled on biological evolution.

Feedback Loop

A system structure in which the output of a process is fed back as input to the same process, enabling regulation, learning, or runaway behaviour depending on its sign and strength. Ubiquitous in nature and in well-designed software.

Fitness Function

A measure of how well a candidate solution performs in an evolutionary algorithm; the digital analogue of survival-and-reproduction in biology.

Hebbian Learning

The principle that simultaneously active neurons strengthen the connection between them. Often summarised as "cells that fire together wire together."

Hexagram

A six-line figure in the I Ching, built of solid (yang) and broken (yin) lines. The sixty-four hexagrams form an early binary notation, pre-dating electronic computing by roughly three millennia.

I Ching (Yijing)

The "Book of Changes," a Chinese divinatory and philosophical text (oldest layers c. 1000 BCE). Its sixty-four hexagrams are built from binary trigrams and inspired Leibniz's 1703 essay on binary arithmetic.

Innate Immunity

The fast, broad, non-specific first layer of the immune system; the biological analogue of a perimeter firewall and heuristic rule set.

Koan

A short paradoxical question or story used in Chan/Zen practice to exhaust the rational mind and provoke insight. Often cited as an analogue for questions in engineering that resist their first obvious answer.

Laozi (Lao Tzu)

Semi-legendary Chinese philosopher (c. 6th century BCE), traditional author of the Dao De Jing. His teachings on wu wei and the natural grain of things underlie much of Daoist and later Chan/Zen thought.

Local Rule, Global Behavior

A hallmark of complex adaptive systems: rich patterns that emerge when many agents follow simple rules based only on information available in their immediate neighbourhood.

Mandala

A circular diagram used in Hindu and Buddhist traditions as a symbolic map of the cosmos and an aid to meditation. From the Sanskrit for "circle" or "community."

Multi-Agent System

A system composed of many agents that interact with each other and with a shared environment, often producing collective intelligence.

Neural Architecture Search (NAS)

The automated discovery of neural network architectures, typically using evolutionary or reinforcement-learning techniques.

Neuroplasticity

The capacity of the brain to change its structure and wiring throughout life in response to experience, learning, or injury.

Niṣkāma Karma

"Desireless action": the Gītā's principle of acting in accordance with dharma without attachment to outcomes. A framing that prefigures modern discussions of AI alignment, reward hacking, and process-over-outcome evaluation.

Nyāya

A classical school of Indian logic founded by Gautama (c. 2nd century BCE). Its five-member syllogism (pratijñā, hetu, udāharaṇa, upanaya, nigamana) is an early formalisation of chain-of-thought reasoning.

Pāṇini

Ancient Indian grammarian (c. 5th century BCE) whose Aṣṭādhyāyī formalised Sanskrit with a system of rules, metarules, and exceptions that anticipates later work in formal language theory.

Patañjali

Ancient author of the Yoga Sūtras, a concise text (c. 200 BCE–400 CE) systematising yogic practice. Its account of attention (dhāraṇā, dhyāna, samādhi) is a precursor to modern attention mechanisms.

Piṅgala

Ancient Indian scholar (c. 3rd–2nd century BCE) whose Chandahśāstra introduced binary encoding of metrical patterns and an early account of the Fibonacci sequence.

Pratītya-samutpāda

The Buddhist doctrine of "dependent origination": every phenomenon arises in dependence on multiple causes and conditions; nothing exists in isolation. A clean philosophical description of what engineers call a dependency graph.

Reward Hacking

The phenomenon in which an AI system discovers and exploits shortcuts that technically maximise its reward signal while violating the spirit of the task. A practical cautionary tale for any team writing objective functions.

Robustness

The degree to which a system continues to perform acceptably in the face of perturbation, drift, or partial failure. One of the properties nature exhibits most strongly and modern AI still struggles to match.

Self vs Non-Self

The immune-system's fundamental discrimination between the body's own cells and everything else; the security analogue is identity, authentication, and trust.

Self-Organisation

The process by which a system spontaneously develops ordered structure or behaviour without an external controller. Central to biology, to swarm intelligence, and to much recent work on emergent capabilities in AI.

Shoshin

Japanese for "beginner's mind." A Zen ideal of approaching familiar problems with the openness of someone encountering them for the first time. Culturally analogous to preserving exploration in a reinforcement-learning agent.

Shunya / Śūnya

Sanskrit for "zero" or "void." Indian mathematicians gave śūnya positional and conceptual weight centuries before the idea reached Europe; its Buddhist cousin śūnyatā names the emptiness-of-self that grounds dependent origination.

Sparsity

The property of having most values be zero (or negligible). Neurons fire sparsely; efficient AI models increasingly exploit sparsity for speed and power.

Stigmergy

Coordination through modifications of a shared environment, such as pheromone trails left by ants. A powerful model for lightweight, decentralised coordination in multi-agent AI.

Sūtra

"Thread" or "aphoristic rule"; a compressed form in which classical Indian texts (Pāṇini, Patañjali, Nyāya, etc.) encode dense systems of thought in minimal tokens — a deeply algorithmic prose style.

Swarm Intelligence

Collective intelligence arising from many simple agents following local rules without central coordination.

Symbiosis

A long-term, close biological relationship between organisms of different species. A useful frame for designing integrations between software systems that depend on each other.

Wu Wei

Chinese for "non-forcing" or "effortless action." Not passivity but precision about where to push and where to yield. Maps onto backoff algorithms, graceful degradation, and alignment-with-the-grain in systems design.

Yantra

A geometric diagram used in tantric traditions as a meditation device. Unlike a mandala, a yantra is primarily composed of straight lines and geometric figures (triangles, squares, circles).

Yoga Sūtras

Patañjali's 196-sūtra treatise on the theory and practice of yoga. Its eight-limbed path (aṣṭāṅga) includes progressively deeper stages of concentration that parallel modern ideas of attention allocation.

Zero-Trust Architecture

A security model in which no actor is inherently trusted; every request is authenticated and authorised at every boundary. Biologically analogous to continuous immune checkpoints.

Zhengming

Chinese for "the rectification of names." Confucius's doctrine that clear thinking and good governance depend on naming things correctly. The ancient cousin of modern specifications, type systems, and ontologies.

Zhuangzi

Chinese philosopher (c. 4th century BCE) and a foundational Daoist text bearing his name. Known for vivid parables, including the story of the cook whose blade stays sharp for nineteen years by always finding the natural joints of the ox.

Further Reading

This book is an introduction, not an encyclopedia. The works below are excellent next steps for readers who want to go deeper into any of the themes we explored. Each short category opens with a note on why these books, specifically, are the right next step.

On Nature and Computation

The following three are a good trio for a reader who wants to sharpen the general claim of this book — that nature behaves, in important ways, like a computational process — without committing to a single discipline.

- Melanie Mitchell, Complexity: A Guided Tour — a highly readable introduction to complex adaptive systems, and a good bridge from intuition into formal models.
- Stuart Kauffman, At Home in the Universe — on self-organisation and the origin of order; especially strong on why complexity can arise without a designer.
- Geoffrey West, Scale — on the universal scaling laws that link biology, cities, and companies, and on what they say about the limits of growth.

On Evolution and AI

These two books between them make the strongest case that the evolutionary loop is not merely a biological phenomenon but a general-purpose search algorithm.

- Richard Dawkins, The Blind Watchmaker — a classic exposition of evolution as an algorithmic process, and the book that most clearly separates selection from design.

- Kenneth Stanley and Joel Lehman, Why Greatness Cannot Be Planned — on open-ended evolutionary search and novelty-driven learning; a quiet rebuke to over-specified objectives.

On Swarms and Collective Behavior

If Chapter 3 resonated with you, these are the authors to turn to next. They are the people whose work made multi-agent AI possible in the first place.

- Deborah Gordon, Ant Encounters — on how colonies coordinate through local interactions, from one of the field's most accessible writers.
- Iain Couzin and collaborators, papers on collective animal behavior — foundational reading for multi-agent AI designers; start with any of his review articles.

On Brains and Machine Learning

Two books that together map, from different angles, the still-open question of how close our artificial neurons are to the real thing.

- Jeff Hawkins, A Thousand Brains — a theory of neocortical function and its implications for AI, written by an engineer turned neuroscientist.
- Terrence Sejnowski, The Deep Learning Revolution — the history and the biological roots of modern AI, from someone who lived through most of it.

On Immunity and Cybersecurity

One technical, one accessible. Read in either order.

- Philip Lieberman (ed.), How the Immune System Recognizes Self and Non-Self — primary literature for the curious reader; dense but rewarding.

- Ross Anderson, Security Engineering — the standard reference in the field, with useful ecological framings throughout.

On Ecosystems, Philosophy, and Future AI

Two complementary books that take seriously the idea that intelligence is shaped by environment and embodiment.

- Fritjof Capra and Pier Luigi Luisi, The Systems View of Life — a grand synthesis of systems thinking across scales; useful for reframing organisations as living systems.
- Brian Cantwell Smith, The Promise of Artificial Intelligence — on what reckoning and judgment mean, and why AI still lacks them; an unusually careful philosophical treatment.

On Indian Thought and AI

If Chapter 9 was your first exposure to any of these Indian traditions, the books below are a good, ordered reading path. Start with the Bhagavad Gita rendering for accessibility; move to Plofker or Joseph for the mathematics; approach Panini and the Nyaya texts last, when a little context will help.

- S. M. Katre, Aṣṭādhyāyī of Pāṇini — an accessible English translation of the foundational Sanskrit grammar, with commentary.

- George Cardona, Pāṇini: A Survey of Research — the standard scholarly survey of Pāṇinian studies and their relevance to linguistics and computation.
- Edwin F. Bryant, The Yoga Sūtras of Patañjali — a careful translation with extensive classical commentary on attention, concentration, and meditation.
- Eknath Easwaran, The Bhagavad Gita — a widely-read modern English rendering of the Gītā; especially useful for its treatment of niṣkāma karma.
- B. K. Matilal, The Character of Logic in India — a scholarly account of Nyāya logic and Indian epistemology.
- George Gheverghese Joseph, The Crest of the Peacock: Non-European Roots of Mathematics — on Indian contributions to algorithmic mathematics, including śūnya and Piṅgala's binary work.
- Kim Plofker, Mathematics in India — a rigorous technical history of Indian mathematics from 500 BCE to 1800 CE.
- Padmanabh S. Jaini, The Jaina Path of Purification — for readers interested in Jain anekāntavāda and its epistemology of multiple standpoints.
- Subhash Kak, The Wishing Tree: Presence and Promise of India — essays on computation, language, and cognition in Indian intellectual history.
- Michael Witzel and Stephanie Jamison (various), essays on early Sanskrit texts — foundational academic scholarship for those who want to go to primary sources.

On Chinese Thought and Systems Thinking

These are approachable entries into the Chinese classical traditions covered in Chapter 9. Start with the D. C. Lau or Ames/Hall rendering of the Dao De Jing for the Daoist current, move to the Analects for the Confucian one, and read Needham when you want the long history of Chinese science alongside.

- Laozi, Dao De Jing — recommended translations: D. C. Lau (Penguin Classics), Roger T. Ames and David L. Hall, and Stephen Mitchell for a freer poetic rendering.
- Confucius, The Analects — recommended translations: D. C. Lau (Penguin Classics) and Edward Slingerland's more scholarly edition with commentary.
- Zhuangzi, The Complete Works — Burton Watson's translation remains the most-cited English edition; Brook Ziporyn's is more recent and philosophically precise.
- Richard Wilhelm (trans.), The I Ching or Book of Changes — the standard English edition, with a famous foreword by C. G. Jung; a useful read alongside Leibniz's binary essay.
- Joseph Needham, Science and Civilisation in China — the monumental multi-volume history of Chinese science and technology; even one volume repays a careful reading.
- Benjamin Schwartz, The World of Thought in Ancient China — a synoptic account of Confucian, Daoist, Mohist, and Legalist strands of early Chinese philosophy.

On Buddhist and Zen Thought

These three work as a single arc — from plain beginner's-mind instruction to the philosophical underpinnings of emptiness and dependent origination.

- Shunryu Suzuki, Zen Mind, Beginner's Mind — the classic introduction to Zen practice; source of the phrase "beginner's mind."
- Thich Nhat Hanh, The Heart of the Buddha's Teaching — a warm and lucid explanation of dependent origination, emptiness, and the Four Noble Truths.
- Jay L. Garfield, The Fundamental Wisdom of the Middle Way — Nagarjuna's classical treatment of śūnyatā (emptiness), with scholarly commentary; a bridge from meditation into formal philosophy.

End of book.

www.ingramcontent.com/pod-product-compliance
Lightning Source LLC
LaVergne TN
LVHW100323210926
848480LV00003B/1229